How the Hot Dog
Found Its Bun

How the Hot Dog Found Its Bun

Accidental Discoveries *and* Unexpected Inspirations That Shape What We Eat *and* Drink

Josh Chetwynd

illustrations by **David Cole Wheeler**

LYONS PRESS
Guilford, Connecticut
An imprint of Globe Pequot Press

For Jennifer and Becca

Lyons Press is an imprint of Globe Pequot Press.

Illustrations: David Cole Wheeler
Text design: Ann Pawlick
Project editor: Julie Marsh
Layout: Maggie Peterson

Library of Congress Cataloging-in-Publication Data is available on file.

ISBN 978-0-7627-7750-1
Printed in the United States of America
10 9 8 7 6 5 4 3 2 1

Contents

CONTENTS

Drinks

Kitchen Inventions and Innovations

Introduction

Luck touches every part of our lives. As the Roman poet Ovid once said, "Luck affects everything; let your hook always be cast. In the stream where you least expect it, there will be a fish."

In the culinary world, hearing luck and food in the same sentence isn't always a good thing. It can conjure up thoughts like, "You're lucky you didn't get sick from that week-old pizza!" But when it comes to the *creation* of great dishes, satisfying drinks, and useful kitchen utensils, it's a concept that can captivate us.

Consider, if you will, the Reese's Peanut Butter Cup. Back in the 1970s and 1980s, the chocolate-peanut-butter marriage was celebrated with a highly successful ad campaign featuring two people colliding and their beloved foods intermingling. Their campy verbal exchange— "You got peanut butter on my chocolate!" "Your chocolate is in my peanut butter!"—would end with unintended gastronomic bliss. Decades on, these spots still resonate (for proof, just check out a parody of the ads on YouTube from the animated comedy series *Family Guy*). Why? Because we love happy culinary accidents, and, as it happens, there's no shortage of them. Nachos and Popsicles. French dip sandwiches and potato chips. Microwaves and paper towels.

Luck, in fact, is the resonating theme of this book. It drives so many of those culinary instances of unforeseen good fortune that have kept our bellies full and our kitchens running smoothly over the centuries.

Behind these lucky discoveries are usually acts of *serendipity*, a concept first coined by Horace Walpole in 1754. He'd read a book about Serendip (modern-day Sri Lanka) called *The Three Princes of Serendip* and was fascinated by the title characters, who "were always making discoveries, by accident and sagacity, of things which they were not in quest of." Using that quote as a definition, he started describing some of his work as *serendipity*.

What makes serendipity so fascinating is the combination of the lucky find and the smarts (or to use Walpole's fancier term *sagacity*) to capitalize on the breakthrough. As Albert Einstein once said about discovery: "The really valuable factor is intuition. . . . There is only the way of intuition, which is helped by a feeling for the order lying behind the appearance." The *intuition* to turn what looks like a blunder into something special comes up often throughout this book. Take the ever-popular cereal Wheaties for instance. A fella was cooking up some gruel when a bit dripped onto an open stove, crackling over the open fire. He could have simply cleaned the mess and gone about his day. But he intuitively recognized its potential and brought it to a local company, which, employing a little sagacity of its own, figured out how to transform the flakes into a commercially viable way to eat breakfast.

While the book mines many stories of serendipity, *chance* does come in other forms—and these get play here as well. For instance, there are times when you actually know exactly what you want to create but struggle with how to get there. When happenstance allows you to find that missing link, these moments have been dubbed by scientist and author Royston M. Roberts as *pseudoserendipity*. For those who have ever popped a couple of Alka-Seltzer tablets for soothing relief after an exceptionally rich meal or a little too much alcohol, you can chalk it up to this particular form of fantastic luck. An inventor plugged away looking for just the right combination to make the famed tablet but came up empty until a trip to the local newspaper surprisingly presented the answers to his problem.

Just for good measure, I've also covered a third type of fluky creation. It's not so much serendipity as it is about unpredictable or mistaken motivations (call them the cousins of serendipity). These occur before the first physical steps of creation, coming during the conceptualization phase. They include either an unplanned fortuitous encounter that spurs the essential kernel of the idea or a completely misguided reason to start rolling up the sleeves. For example, the Filet-O-Fish falls in the category of unanticipated inspirations. A McDonald's franchisee was all about making burgers, but when he found out the surprising reason for why he was doing terrible business on Fridays (thanks to churchgoers who didn't eat meat on this day), he was forced to come up with an alternative to the regular menu. As for the misguided, there was Sylvester Graham, who created his eponymous crackers because he hoped eating them would help diminish sex drives.

So what exactly draws us to these culinary origin stories in which luck features so prominently? First off, the stories are entertaining and surprising. Often the initial steps for products like Tabasco Sauce or cheese puffs are far from what you'd anticipate. Also, in some ways, discovering just how much fate plays in the recipe of so many successful products is inspirational. It gives hope to toiling chefs or tinkerers that if they keep trying long enough lady luck may ultimately lend a difference-making hand.

Interestingly, these two reasons have led to another common phenomenon when it comes to accidental discoveries and unexpected inspirations in the kitchen: myth making. It turns out that a number of highly heralded anecdotes of this type of invention are untrue. In a way, this seems counterintuitive because what inventor would want to weave a tall tale that gives greater applause to a mistake than to its creator? (Don't we all want full credit?) Part of the explanation is that quite often it's not the original inventor who spins the fanciful yarn but future beneficiaries who see the story as a memorable way to bring attention to the product. If the story inspires or is captivating enough to increase interest why not stretch the truth?

Throughout this book I've tried to do a little food-myth-busting by flagging those stories, assessing their accuracy, and, when appropriate, serving up alternate creation explanations. Still, even if some of these accounts are more fanciful than honest histories, they remain worthy to recount. Why? Because more often than not they've become a central part of a certain food or drink's narrative. For example, maple-syrup makers often cite a historical tale that's probably apocryphal; ditto for ice-cream cone producers. While those legends may not tell you the full story of the products' beginnings, they do give you some insight into how the products have been marketed over the years and how they became such an indelible part of our everyday lives.

Starters and Small Plates

Bisquick: Tardy train traveler

Timing—or the lack thereof—is everything. The phrase may be cliché, but for Carl Smith it was the key to discovering one of the baking world's most versatile products. One November night in 1930, Smith, a General Mills executive, hopped onto a Southern Pacific Railroad train in Portland, Oregon. He was returning home to San Francisco and was pretty hungry. Alas, it was late and formal meals had long since been served in the dining car. He resigned himself to the fact that he'd have to take whatever scraps were left at such an hour.

Yet, he was astonished to find himself quickly being served fresh, delicious hot biscuits. If he'd been feasting during a designated eating time, he wouldn't have given it much thought as the train's kitchen would have been expected to have biscuits good to go. But enjoying such a treat at an odd hour piqued his curiosity. He headed back into the galley and asked how the chef had such fantastic flakey delights at the ready. The cook took Smith to an ice box and showed him the secret: The dough (a combination of lard, flour, baking powder, and salt) had been mixed beforehand and kept cold in order to be baked at a moment's notice.

Smith immediately realized having biscuits that could be prepared so quickly was a winning idea. Upon returning home, he went to General Mills' team of chemists and challenged them to come up with a mixture that could yield biscuits comparable to those he'd had on his trip back to San Francisco. Actually, Smith took it one step further: He wanted them to taste homemade. It wouldn't be an easy task. Typical shortenings such as lard or butter would be problematic in a mass-produced mix because they wouldn't keep well on grocery shelves. Following much consideration, they opted for sesame oil, which didn't go rancid after sitting for a long time. Even after settling on the right oil, the scientists labored hard trying to put together the right combination of ingredients to ensure that the biscuits would come out perfectly.

Testing was done in spy-level secrecy. Though Smith had only happened upon the idea after a late entry into a dining car, the General Mills folks were convinced that others would quickly identify the commercial value of such a mix. They were right. Bisquick (a moniker that combined "biscuit" and "quick") rolled out in 1931 and within a short time there were ninety-five other brands for sale. Only six survived the first year, with Bisquick dominating the market. Part of the reason for Bisquick's popularity was kitchen mavens everywhere understood that the mix could be used for more than just making biscuits. Everything from coffee cakes and pancakes to cheeseburger pies (my personal favorite example of pure decadence) were being created with the invention.

General Mills zealously marketed the product, successfully employing giveaways (free tins were included early on), celebrity endorsers (Shirley Temple hawked Bisquick for a while), special clubs (the popular Bisquick Recipe Club provided cookbooks and encouraged recipe sharing), and even a dash of sexual politics (a 1940s motto was "so simple, even a husband can do it"). It also inspired other companies to innovate all sorts of baking mixes. Without Bisquick, it might have been years before somebody came up with those yummy easy-to-make chocolate cakes. But the biggest selling point for Bisquick was its original promise that it would only take ninety seconds to make biscuits from the box to the oven—proving once again that timing is everything.

Brown 'n Serve Rolls: Fire alarm discovery

For housewives in post–World War II suburbia, Brown 'n Serve Rolls were a go-to staple. Partially cooked and kept in the refrigerator, these babies, which have no relation to popular Brown 'N Serve sausages, could be popped in the oven and in just seven minutes put on the table hot and fluffy. In an era before the invention of microwave ovens, this was one of the first food items that could be cooked with almost no preparation at home and still taste restaurant quality.

Joe Gregor, who owned a small bakery in Avon Park, Florida, knew he needed a game-changing product. His business wasn't doing so well, and the few patrons who came in explained they wanted bread products for home that could be oven-fresh. Gregor got the picture and spent hours with his buddy Jules Jacobsen trying to come up with a partially cooked roll that could be reheated at home.

Gregor's efforts yielded nothing but failure until a fire literally sparked discovery. In truth, it wasn't an inferno but a fire alarm that did the trick. You see, the civic-minded Gregor was more than just a baker—he was also a volunteer fireman. One afternoon in the late 1940s, he heard the town's fire bell sound. He was right in the middle of baking some rolls, but he knew he had to run. So Gregor prematurely pulled the dough out of the oven (to avoid a fire of his own) and headed off to take care of the emergency. When he got to the scene, it turned out that there wasn't a big blaze—just a small brush fire—and Gregor was sent home.

Much to his surprise, when he got back to the bakery he discovered his unfinished rolls hadn't fallen. Typically when bread is pulled out of the oven early it won't keep its shape, but these did. Why, he wondered? It turned out to be pure luck. The oven had been leaking heat. Instead of cooking at 450°F the way Gregor intended, it only got up to 275°F. The lower temperature had kept the rolls standing tall. Even better news: When the rolls were put back in the oven for just a few minutes, they came out tasting great.

The new creation—originally called Pop-n-Oven rolls—were a hit locally, catching the attention of General Mills. In 1949 the big food company paid $60,000 for the recipe, and by September 1950 *Popular Science* magazine was touting Gregor's work as "nationally famous." At first General Mills tried to keep Gregor's process under wraps. They even gave the rolls a sci-fi–esque code name: Project 49. But over time, in an effort to spur flour sales, the company shifted gears providing commercial bakers with thermometers and instructions on how to make the half-cooked items. While General Mills stopped producing Brown 'n Serve rolls by the 1970s, partially cooked rolls can still be found in supermarkets (Wal-Mart sells multiple brands in twelve-roll packs) thanks to a community-conscious baker and his busted oven.

Buffalo Wings: Late night munchies

In a way, Buffalo wings come from exactly where you'd expect them to originate: at a bar, late at night, with a group of young (possibly inebriated) guys. Still, neither the dish's inventor nor the guys who first laid their eyes on the eventual pub favorite had any idea that they were going to be a part of something special that evening.

It was 1964 on a Friday night in late October and six friends in Buffalo, New York, got out of a Paul Newman movie (likely *The Outrage*) and headed over to the Anchor Bar. Their buddy, Dominic Bellissimo, was the son of Anchor owners Frank and Teressa, and, though it was 11:30 p.m., they figured it was a good place to finish off the night. Fellas being fellas, the group wanted two things: food and drink. Whether they boozed is unclear, but the group persisted enough about the grub to force chef Teressa to come up with something.

The problem: It was late and Teressa didn't really have anything going. Surveying the kitchen, she noticed some small chicken wings. At the time, these trifles really had just one destination in a kitchen—a stock pot to become part of a soup or stew. But Teressa took what she had and broiled (some say deep-fried) the little wings. According to Dominic, his mom used the chicken, in part, because it would have been a shame to consign such lovely wings to a soupy end. She then added some margarine and threw on some Frank's Original Red Hot Sauce that happened to be in the kitchen. A popular brand in western New York, Frank's (no connection to Frank Bellissimo) is a combo of "aged cayenne red peppers, vinegar, salt, and garlic."

Upon seeing the plates of basted wings, one of the buddies, Don Zanghi, asked, "What are these?" Another friend replied: "I don't know, but we better eat." Zanghi wasn't sure how to attack the small-but-meaty morsels. He looked at Anchor owner Frank Bellissimo and said, "Frank, there's no silverware." Maybe Frank was a trailblazer—or more likely he was tired and wanted to end the conversation—but his terse answer set sail the how-to etiquette for Buffalo wings. He said, "Keep quiet and use your fingers!"

The dish became the toast of Buffalo and beyond. In 1977 the city proclaimed July 29 Chicken Wing Day. Nineteen years later, a special Frank & Teressa's Original Anchor Bar Buffalo Chicken Wing Sauce came out. It's similar to Frank's Original Red Hot Sauce, but includes margarine, spices, and natural gums in its recipe. There's even a National Buffalo Wing Festival, complete with a Hall of Flame honoring Buffalo Wing greats. Sure enough, Teressa and Frank were inaugural inductees in 2006. Teressa is so revered that the following year one Buffalo man carved an oak statue in her likeness.

Although Frank and Teressa have long since passed on, the Anchor continues to profit from their creation. In 2009 the bar was selling 2,000 pounds of chicken wings *a day*.

Caesar Salad: Empty refrigerator

As strange as it might sound, the Caesar salad was a dish born in Mexico. It wasn't named after Julius Caesar, but after its creator, an Italian immigrant to the United States. The likely source of inspiration: kitchen scraps and leftovers. And, if that wasn't befuddling enough, the dish was meant to be eaten with the hands rather than with a fork.

Caesar Cardini is most often credited with producing this dish dubbed by Paris's International Society of Epicures in 1953 as "the greatest recipe to originate from the Americas in fifty years." Cardini moved to America from Italy's Lake Maggiore area as a young man. When prohibition hit in 1920, he saw a great opportunity for a new business. While living in San Diego he crossed the border into Mexico and opened up a hotel and restaurant in Tijuana. Down south, guests could sidestep the alcohol ban and have good food with some potent spirits. Hotel Caesar lured not only San Diego socialites but also Hollywood stars. Among those who made the trip to Cardini's establishment were W. C. Fields, Jean Harlow, and Clark Gable.

Needless to say, during holidays—when people wanted to celebrate with a strong drink—the place was a madhouse. July 4, 1924 was one such day. Miscalculating the amount of food he needed, Cardini found his kitchen short on supplies. The story goes that he improvised with what was left, throwing together romaine lettuce, eggs, garlic, croutons, Parmesan cheese, olive oil, and Worcestershire sauce (and possibly a few other items, including lemon juice). Rather than cutting up the lettuce, Cardini presented the dish as a main course with customers picking up whole leaves of romaine in their hands and eating.

The combination enthralled the glitterati and Caesar's became a pilgrimage spot for foodies. So much so that none other than Julia Child headed down to Mexico with her family to experience Caesar's creation. In her book, *From Julia Child's Kitchen*, the famed writer and chef talked giddily of the trip. She wrote: "One of my early remembrances of restaurant life was going to Tijuana in 1925 or 1926 with my parents, who were wildly excited that they should finally lunch at Caesar's Restaurant." Child recounts Cardini himself mixing the dressing for the salad at her family's table (an act he typically did for patrons).

Not surprisingly with a dish as wonderful as the Caesar salad, its genesis became a hotly contested claim. The assertion that a cook from Chicago invented it in 1903 is generally disregarded, but a more serious challenge comes from Cardini's own brother, Alex, a former pilot. According to his son and granddaughter, Alex, who worked with Caesar (and also at his own restaurant), whipped up the salad for some Air Force buddies down from San Diego one morning in 1926 after a rough night. In honor of the flyboys, he called it the Aviator Salad.

In a 1973 interview published in the *Canadian Magazine*, Alex staked his claim. He said he invented the salad first—an impromptu creation made following a lunch discussion with his partner Paul Maggiora. At the same time, Alex didn't deny his brother had his own leafy handiwork. "One day, my brother Caesar said to me, 'Everybody talks about your salad,' so he made one too," Alex explained. "Customers used to go to Caesar's place for Caesar's salad and to Paul and me for mine."

Most food historians split the difference, giving Caesar praise for coming up with the basic salad in 1924 and Alex glory for the ever-popular addition of anchovies. I have no ties to either of the Cardini men, but Child's story of traveling to Tijuana to try an already popular dish in 1925 or 1926 appears to predate Alex's claim to the dish, giving Caesar some support in this fraternal salad disagreement.

Cheese: Not your average bag

Sometimes when discussing food origins—particularly with items that were accidentally discovered—you have to ask yourself: Who was the brave and/or crazy person who took that initial taste? The first person to take a bite of cheese falls squarely in this category.

We don't know the name of that bold man or woman, but the valiant sampler was almost certainly a prehistoric herder. Cave paintings indicate animal milking occurred in the Libyan Sahara around or before 5000 BC. Another archeological find suggests similar activity in modern Switzerland in approximately 6000 BC. In later centuries, men shepherding goats, sheep, and cows would often store milk in pouches made from animal stomachs (hey, nothing went to waste back then). One part of these beasts' bellies, called the abomasum, was full of a substance known as rennet. When the milk sat a little too long in the pouches, the rennet went to work creating chunks, known as curds, along with leftover liquid, aka whey.

I'm sure the coagulated bits didn't smell good. Yet somebody took a piece—hopefully with some alcohol (alas, there weren't any good pinot noirs at the time)—and gave it a shot. It wasn't half bad and people began to recognize that if you drained the liquid and dried out the chunks, it kept quite well and could be stored for later eating. (Geek note: Early history gave us a number of accidental discoveries, including bread and beer; I'm giving cheese the love here because compared with that other fare, scarfing prehistoric fromage was surely a far greater gastronomic leap of faith.)

Salt was an early ingredient used to add flavor. As a result, some historians believe that the first cheeses were similar to the brine-cured feta we might find at a fine grocer today. Egyptian, Greek, and Roman cultures matured the cheese-making process, and by the Middle Ages wedges of the stuff were part of European diets. The great king Charlemagne was said to be a big fan—though it's unclear if he got hooked after trying early Brie or some Roquefort.

In terms of the art of cheese-making, cultures recognized over time that the abomasum was key in the production of cheese so pieces of that part of the animal stomach were sliced, salted, and dried. They were then added to milk to create curds. For those who find that process stomach turning, you'll be happy to know that nowadays genetically engineered bacteria are often set up in vats to produce the necessary curdling agent.

As for the quantity of milk necessary to make cheese, it takes approximately eight pounds of milk to produce one pound of cheese.

Cobb Salad: Celebrity restaurateur

During the golden age of Hollywood, The Brown Derby restaurants were the movie industry's unofficial canteens. Shirley Temple had her tenth birthday at one. Ronald Reagan chose a Derby for his final meal before shipping off for service during World War II. In an episode of *I Love Lucy*, Lucille Ball's character headed to the restaurant's Hollywood location on a trip to Los Angeles to scope out movie stars because she said it was "their watering hole." As famed movie director Cecil B. DeMille put it in a 1943 telegram: The Derby was "the most famous restaurant in the world."

At the center of this starry constellation of celebrities was Bob Cobb. Originally hired in 1926 to run the first Derby, Cobb would go on to own the restaurant's four star-studded locations throughout L.A. The most famous one, which was just off Hollywood Boulevard and Vine Street, helped make that intersection internationally known. Cobb was more than just a restaurateur—he was also a close friend to practically every mover and shaker in town. In 1938 he led a group that included luminaries Bing Crosby, Barbara Stanwyck, Gary Cooper, George Burns, and Walt Disney in bringing a high-level minor league baseball team to Los Angeles. Appropriately, the club was named the Hollywood Stars.

Still, all his rubbing elbows with the superstars didn't cause Cobb to lose focus on his real job: running restaurants. This was practically a round-the-clock responsibility as, at least in the beginning, The Derby offered twenty-four-hour service.

It was the combination of those long days and Cobb's influential friends that produced the Cobb Salad. In the late 1920s, Cobb wearily entered the kitchen in the wee hours one night. Cobb was famished but wasn't too thrilled with his choices. In the early going, The Derby's menu was pretty limited to such simple dishes as hamburgers, hot dogs, grilled cheese sandwiches, and chili. Cobb wanted something different and pulled out whatever leftovers he could find to avoid the same-old, same-old menu choices. Because he was tired, Cobb went for something that could be prepared simply. He chopped up some lettuce, chicken, and a few other ingredients and started munching.

He was in the midst of his impromptu salad when four Hollywood bigwigs, including studio mogul Jack Warner (of Warner Bros. fame) and Sid Grauman (founder of Hollywood's Chinese Theatre), checked in on their buddy after seeing a film preview. The men liked the look of Cobb's meal and asked for their own plates of what was intended to be a one-off concoction.

Those in the know began ordering the off-menu salad almost immediately. But Cobb waited to add it to the menu until he'd perfected his unplanned masterpiece. The final dish featured finely chopped chicken breast, iceberg lettuce, romaine, watercress, chicory, chives, tomatoes, avocados, bacon, hard-boiled eggs, Roquefort cheese, and french dressing. When Cobb opened up the Hollywood Derby in 1929, the Cobb Salad finally became an official menu item. Although The Brown Derby restaurants no longer exist in L.A., the Cobb Salad remains a worldwide star.

Kellogg's Corn Flakes: Distracted, disagreeable brothers

Will Keith "W. K." Kellogg had it tough in the early years of his life. He left school after sixth grade and held a number of menial jobs. As a twenty-four-year-old, he dourly wrote in his diary, "I feel kind of blue . . . Am afraid that I will always be a poor man the way things look now." His older brother, John Harvey, added to his pangs of inferiority. A renowned doctor, John Harvey set up a hospital and health spa called The Battle Creek Sanitarium in Battle Creek, Michigan, which was *the* place for many of America's elite looking to get fit in the late nineteenth and early twentieth centuries. Noted guests included Henry Ford, Thomas Edison, J. C. Penney, and President William H. Taft.

W. K. would eventually go to work for his brother, which was a pretty humiliating endeavor. W. K. made a paltry six dollars a week at the Sanitarium, never earning more than eighty-seven dollars a month during his twenty-five years on the job. He apparently wasn't allowed to go on vacation until he'd worked there for seven years. His responsibilities ranged from balancing the books and running the organization's mail-order business to shining his brother's shoes and giving him shaves.

Thankfully for W. K., fate intervened in an unexpected way. A Seventh-day Adventist, Dr. John Harvey Kellogg had religious convictions that required him to focus intently on producing food that was good for the body. At the heart of many of the Sanitarium's creations were grains. This even included trying to produce a grain alternative to coffee. Among the other efforts was a more digestible substitute for basic bread. It was during this process that W. K. got his big break.

In 1894 the pair was experimenting with boiling wheat dough. During the process they were called away. When they came back, the dough had dried out. Nevertheless, they put the stale stuff through rollers with the hopes it would still be transformed into a long flat sheet of dough. Instead, the result was a bevy of small wheat flakes. The Sanitarium's patients loved the invention, which they called *Granose*.

W. K. saw a chance to make his mark. Dr. Kellogg wasn't as enthused. The doctor wouldn't even give his brother space for a proper factory to develop the discovery. Still, the resourceful W. K. was able to produce and sell 113,400 pounds of the cereal in 1896. With a little more tinkering, the brothers found replacing wheat with corn as the basis for the flakes offered an even tastier option. Called *Sanitas Toasted Corn Flakes*, the new cereal continued to do the business.

It was time for W. K. to move out of his brother's shadow—though he did it with some trepidation. W. K. waited until Dr. Kellogg went on an extended trip to Europe and built a proper factory in 1900. The elder Kellogg wasn't happy upon his return, insisting that W. K. reimburse him $50,000 in construction costs.

The big rift finally came during another one of Dr. Kellogg's trips to Europe. (For all his education, the good doctor clearly didn't realize these trips weren't such a good idea.) W. K. decided that the only way to expand the market for his corn flakes was to add sugar. For Dr. Kellogg, this was sacrilegious. Sugar was one of the ingredients that served to undermine good health. W. K. insisted and set up his own business, Battle Creek Toasted Corn Flake Company, in 1906. While the pair would remain in business together for some time, squabbling over the product led to lawsuits. In the end the less-educated, but ever scrappy W. K. would win the primary right to use the Kellogg name commercially. By this time W. K. had redubbed his cereal *Kellogg's Corn Flakes* in order to differentiate it in a marketplace full of competitors.

Nachos: Ravenous army wives

Picture a group of typical nacho eaters. You'd probably imagine sports-obsessed men at a bar wearing replica jerseys with the names of their favorite players sewn on the back. Of course there would also be a pitcher of beer on the table. Surprisingly, the first people to enjoy this popular cheese-laden tortilla chip appetizer were far from that image. The original plate of nachos was prepared for a group of proper military officers' wives who were probably more accustomed to a snack of petite sandwiches and tea.

It all happened in 1943 in Piedras Negras, Mexico. The border town was across the Rio Grande River from Eagle Pass, Texas, which during World War II was home to Eagle Pass Army Airfield. For the married women on this US Army Air Force base, crossing the border to shop and enjoy the Mexican culture was a popular diversion.

One day a gaggle of the ladies moseyed over to a Piedras Negras restaurant called the Victory Club. The establishment's maitre d'— Ignacio "Nacho" Anaya—was there to greet them, but he had a big problem: He couldn't locate the cook. Not wanting to turn away the patrons, he put on his chef's hat. He looked around the kitchen and threw together what he had, which according to *The Oxford Companion to American Food and Drink* "consisted of neat canapes of tortilla chips, cheese, and jalapeno peppers." In a dash of irony, Anaya's son would tell the *San Antonio Express-News* in 2002 that the cheese his father used that day was from Wisconsin. He also said that tostados were used to make the first chips. In the years that followed Anaya became the restaurant's head chef—after all, how could you *not* give that job to the man who created nachos? The dish took on Anaya's nickname and was advertised as "Nacho Specials" on both sides of the border.

The combo of chips and melted cheese spread rapidly. By the 1960s it was a popular component of Tex-Mex cuisine. But its place as a global phenomenon owes some tribute to a man named Frank Liberto, who turned nachos into stadium food. In 1977 Liberto unveiled a new nacho concession at Arlington Stadium, home of baseball's Texas Rangers at the time. Because real cheese didn't have a great shelf life (and melting it would require an oven or broiler), Liberto devised a fast food form of Anaya's masterpiece that was part cheese and part secret ingredients. The new sauce didn't need to be heated and, when it came to shelf life, it could likely survive a nuclear blast. Its formula was so hush hush that a twenty-nine-year-old man was arrested in 1983 for trying to buy trade secrets divulging Liberto's formula.

When famed Monday Night Football announcer Howard Cosell tasted Liberto's variation on the nacho theme in 1977, he began talking about it incessantly on air, increasing sales. As for Anaya, his son tried to help him trademark the nacho name years after it became a phenomenon but had no luck. Anaya would go on to run his own restaurant, but he never made big money off his crowd-pleasing creation.

Tapas: Fruit flies

Tapas are such a part of the Spanish lifestyle that there's a word to describe the culture built up around them—*tapeo*. As essayist Alicia Rios explained: "The art of *tapeo* . . . induces states of inspiration and delight, it gives rise to witty banter on trivial topics and the interchange of snippets of juicy gossip." If you happen upon any plaza in Spain on a leisurely afternoon, you're sure to find people enjoying some good wine with plates of the finger food (often featuring such popular local fare as chorizo, Serrano ham, and olives).

Over the year, one of the "trivial topics" that has undoubtedly been debated over tapas is how this tradition first came into being.

One popular legend dates back to the thirteenth century. King Alfonso X of Castile had become ill. As part of his convalescence his doctors insisted that he show restraint when it came to his appetite. He was given small portions to eat with his wine. (Apparently wine was a good tonic for getting well.) Once the monarch recovered he liked the custom so much he required taverns under his dominion to offer small plates of food with wine.

While this story sounds wonderfully regal, the actual origin probably has more practical everyday roots. In this explanation, the arid southern region of Andalusia is the birthplace of tapas. The area is known for its sherry, a must-have aperitif for visiting travelers. Unfortunately for tourists and locals alike, the strong, sweet wine not only attracted drinkers but also insects. Fruit flies would hover around open glasses or, even worse, end up in the alcohol. In addition, the dry conditions meant that dust and dirt could sometimes whip up in a breeze and settle in the glass.

The simple solution was to cover the top of the glass when not drinking. This would prevent the pesky bugs from delving into the drink. Some disagreement exists over what was initially chosen as a cover. The *Joy of Cooking*, which places tapas' modern invention in the nineteenth century, says that tavern owners started off putting bread on the glass—others say that a piece of ham typically served as the barrier. According to domestic maven Martha Stewart, small plates were placed over glasses.

Although this practice began as a protective measure, smart business owners realized that it could also be an inducement. "It became customary for the bar owners to offer a sampling of food on the dish to attract customers, and each bar prepared their house specialty, trying to outdo the competition," Stewart wrote. Supporting this story is the etymology of the word *tapas*. Stemming from the word *tapar* ("to cover") the word is typically translated to mean "lid" or "cover."

Nowadays, every region of Spain has its own specialties for tapas lovers. In Castile there is *montados de lomo* (marinated pork loin and bread) or *morcilla* (a fried black pudding sausage dish). If you go to Galicia you'll find finely prepared octopus or shellfish. Deciding on the best tapas will surely lead to a debate of its own . . . over a bottle of wine and some tapas.

Wheaties: Messy cooking

The Breakfast of Champions was once gruel for the infirm and out-of-shape. A Minneapolis health clinician named Mennen Minniberg was mixing up a batch of hot bran one day in 1921 when some of the stuff dripped out of the vat and onto the stove. The scorching surface went to work on the gruel and the result was a handful of crispy flakes.

Minniberg thought they might have some commercial prospects and headed over to a local flour business called Washburn Crosby Company, which would later become General Mills. The executives at Washburn liked the idea and gave Minniberg use of a laboratory to turn his findings into a marketable commodity. Unfortunately, he failed. The flakes proved far too flakey, grinding down to dust when bagged up for sale.

Wheaties' official website acknowledges a health worker bringing his accidental discovery to the company's attention, but doesn't give his name (whether it be Mr. Minniberg or someone else; some have claimed the man's last name was actually Minnenrode). The company also doesn't confirm he was given a shot at turning his unintentional invention into something more.

Nevertheless, everybody agrees on who turned the clinician's blunder into a breakfast wonder. It was a first-class miller named George Cormack. Educated in Scotland, he'd run mills in Canada and throughout the United States. When presented with bran flakes that couldn't hold up when packaged, he labored tirelessly on an alternative. He came up with thirty-six varieties before settling on just the right formula. A key change: replacing bran with wheat.

The company called the cereal Washburn's Gold Medal Wheat Flakes, rolling it out in 1924. The product wasn't immediately a top seller. Apparently a flashy name didn't entice the masses. Acknowledging the problem, the company asked employees and their families to come up with an alternative title. Though Nutties was considered, they settled on Wheaties. For ultra-trivia geeks, Jane Bausman, the wife of the company's export manager, submitted the winning entry.

Success kicked in when they started advertising. The Breakfast of Champions slogan was introduced on an outfield billboard at a minor league baseball stadium, and athletes started appearing on packaging in 1934. Lou Gehrig was the first. At the 1939 Major League All-Star Game, forty-six of the event's fifty-one players endorsed the cereal. Countless more ballplayers and other athletes offered testimonials over the years about how they adored the wheat flakes. Despite their love for on-field legends, Wheaties initially put these sporting heroes' images on the back of the boxes. It wasn't until 1958, starting with Olympic decathlete Bob Richards, that athletes' pictures started adorning the front.

With the exception of a brief flirtation with kids' radio programming in the early 1950s, General Mills has held tight to Wheaties' athletic focus. So much so that when Ohio's congressional delegation once lobbied the cereal makers to put former astronaut and US senator John Glenn on a box, they were rebuffed. After the September 11, 2001, attacks, Hillary Rodham Clinton wrote the company's president urging him to recognize a New York City police officer and firefighter on a box along with a Port Authority officer. Again, the company passed.

Needless to say, don't expect the faces of George Cormack or Mr. Minniberg on a box anytime soon.

Main Courses

Chicken Marengo: Broken supply line

This popular Italian dish gets its name from a battle in the town of Marengo, just south of Turin. Its inspiration: the famed Napoleon Bonaparte. The great general was elected France's first consul in February 1800 (effectively becoming the leader of the new republic) and was itching to show his might. To that end, his audacious plan was to cross the Alps, enter Italy and overtake the Austrian army. When the two opposing forces engaged on June 14, 1800, things initially looked bad for Napoleon and his men. One of his trusted lieutenants, General Louis Desaix, reportedly told his leader, "This battle is completely lost, but it is only two o'clock; there is time to win another." Though Desaix didn't survive the day, he was right, as the French rallied to prevail at what was dubbed the Battle of Marengo.

Following the clash, Napoleon was well famished. This wasn't surprising as the Corsican had a habit of never eating before a battle. The future monarch's Swiss chef, Dunand, was well aware that his boss was going to want something particularly pleasing after the hard-fought victory. Unfortunately, the typical standbys were going to be impossible to make because the food wagons had been lost during the battle.

Dunand hurriedly sent out soldiers from the quartermaster's staff to forage for supplies. All they could get, according to author Patricia Bunning Stevens, were "three small eggs, four tomatoes, six crayfish, a small hen, a little garlic, and some oil." The chef took the hodgepodge and went to work. He presented Napoleon with sliced chicken browned in oil and flavored with garlic, along with tomatoes, fried eggs, and crayfish on a tin plate. (It's also said by some that a soldier's ration of bread was toasted and added. Others claim it's unlikely that tomatoes were a part of the original dish.) As amazing as the military triumph was, equally surprising was Napoleon's love for the unplanned fare. The first consul supposedly told Dunand, "You must feed me like this after every battle."

Versions of this story have been told in such respected publications as *The Oxford Companion to Food* and *Larousse Gastronomique*. Still, not everyone is a believer. Stevens concedes that the tale is "plausible" but argues "[t]he dish is sheer legend." She points to the fact that Napoleon's private secretary noted in his memoirs that food for that fated meal was supplied by a local convent and that the French received an "abundance of good provisions and wine." (It's worth noting that even if the convent offered lots of food, it could have included the strange combination that forced Dunand to create his funky combo.)

Stevens posits that the story of the dish was a marketing ploy by an unnamed restaurateur who thought a good anecdote would draw more buyers. Whatever the case, the dish itself was one of Napoleon's favorites and may very well have been one he savored his whole life. Even when exiled on St. Helena in his final years, Napoleon was said to have talked often about his great victory at Marengo. He was even buried in the grey overcoat he wore on the day of the battle. As for chicken Marengo, it's outlived the iconic French leader—with some changes. The pan-fried chicken is now often cooked in a white wine sauce, crayfish are rarely served as part of the dish, and mushrooms are a popular addition.

Chicken Tikka Masala: Fussy customer

Forget such evocatively named English dishes as *bangers and mash* or *bubble and squeak*. The United Kingdom's national food is Indian. "Having a curry" (as it's called there) is so popular that Scotland's *Daily Record* newspaper once put the annual spending on Indian food in the United Kingdom at more than four billion dollars.

With that context, it's no wonder that the British take great pride in their contribution to the cuisine. So much so that a member of Parliament once went so far as to ask the European Union to designate one famed Indian dish, Chicken Tikka Masala, as a Scottish creation. It didn't matter that the dish's creator merely stumbled upon it.

Ali Ahmed Asham was a chef at Glasgow's Shish Mahal restaurant in the 1970s. He'd been dealing with a stomach ulcer, according to the *Daily Record*, when one night a customer came in for Chicken Tikka. Asham cooked up the meal, but the patron was not satisfied. He complained that the meat was too dry. An exasperated Asham had a can of Campbell's tomato soup he'd kept on hand to deal with his stomach malady. He

opened it up, added some spices (some say he had already added the spices for his benefit), and sent the chicken out again, but this time with his new sauce. Years after the incident, Asham told a variation on the story minus the drama: "[O]ne day a customer said, 'I'd take some sauce with that, this is a bit dry' so we cooked Chicken Tikka with the sauce, which contains [yogurt], cream, and spices."

Either way, it was a flavorful combo—and one that probably each of the nine thousand curry houses across the United Kingdom serves regularly. To recognize the momentous discovery, Glaswegian member of Parliament Mohammad Sarwar sprung into action in 2009. He made a motion in the British House of Commons regarding "the culinary masterpiece that is Chicken Tikka Masala." Noting that it was "Britain's most popular curry" he asked that his fellow representatives rally around Asham and push the European Union to designate Glasgow as an "EU Protected Designation of Origin" for the dish.

Needless to say Indians didn't like the idea of tomato soup getting acclaim for such a cornerstone option on curry menus.

Zaeemuddin Ahmad, a chef from Delhi's Karim Hotel, maintained that the dish was his family's recipe. "Chicken Tikka Masala is an authentic Mughlai recipe prepared by our forefathers who were royal chefs in the Mughal period," he told Britain's *Daily Telegraph.* "Mughals were avid trekkers and used to spend months altogether in jungles and far off places. They liked roasted form of chicken with spices."

Rahul Verma, an expert on Delhi street food, offered a different opinion, saying the dish was introduced in the Indian region of Punjab in the 1970s. Though he didn't buy Asham's claim, he believed that the dish wasn't by design. "It's basically a Punjabi dish not more than 40 to 50 years old [as of 2009] and must be an accidental discovery which has had periodical improvisation," he said.

While one of those Indian antecedents may very well be true, it's still very possible that the meal Asham produced for his persnickety customer was the one that spawned the Chicken Tikka Masala revolution in Great Britain. As for Britain's leadership, they weren't ready to get behind the cause. Sarwar's effort didn't sit well enough with his colleagues to lead to a formal request to the European Union. In the end only nineteen members of Parliament signed on to his motion.

Chimichanga: Fryer slip-up

The fryer has brought joy to so many cultures around the globe (think french fries or, if you're more adventurous, Scotland's deep-fried haggis). Of course Mexican food has its fair share of deep-fried delicacies with one of its most popular being the chimichanga. Yet despite the cuisine's penchant for greasy fare, this entry into the bubbling goodness was pure happenstance.

For those of you with a weak stomach or limited exposure to the chimichanga, it's effectively a deep-fried burrito—and it's the pride and joy of Tucson, Arizona. A pioneering woman named Monica Flin is widely regarded as the inventor of the dish. Flin, the daughter of a French émigré, opened Tucson's El Charro Café in 1922. Not only was Flin one of the only female restaurant owners in the southern Arizona town, she also practically did it all at the establishment—cooking, serving as hostess, and waiting tables. Throw in the fact that she often had a handful of nieces and nephews hanging around the café, and it's clear that Flin was one busy woman.

One day Flin was in the midst of frying ground beef for tacos. With so much going on, she mistakenly knocked a burrito into the fryer. Her initial reaction was anger and the trilingual woman (she spoke French, Spanish, and English) was on the verge of dishing a popular Spanish "Ch" swear word to express her displeasure. (I'm guessing it was the F-word, Spanish style.) Looking around at some of the children in the kitchen she caught herself at the last moment and blurted out "chimichanga," which translates roughly to the Spanish version of *thingamajig*. As the restaurant's menu says today, "Thankfully for all of us, Monica was a controlled and creative cuss."

The dish, which was once dubbed one of America's top fifty plates by *USA Today*, does have others who claim to be its inventor. Some historians suggest that local Native American tribes or Mexicans on the Sonoran border were frying up burrito-esque meals long before Flin's discovery. George Jacob, owner of another Tucson restaurant called Club 21, said he produced the first fried burrito when a traveler from the east found the traditional type too blah. Jacob slathered it with shortening and used the grill to brown it. The pan-fried creation immediately went on his menu. As Jacob's restaurant didn't open until 1946, it's likely that if he decided the fried burrito was menu worthy, he did so after Flin's folly. Plus, Jacob's original dish wasn't dunked in the deep-fryer. To this day, El Charro still exists with Flin's great-grandniece Carlotta Flores continuing the tradition. She has made a few changes; most notably, lard has been replaced with canola oil in the fryer.

If Flin's story seems familiar to some Midwesterners, it's probably because St. Louis's popular toasted ravioli—deep-fried, meat-filled pasta sprinkled with herbs and grated parmesan cheese—has a similar origin. The most common story about its birth sets the invention's discovery sometime between the 1930s and 1950s at a restaurant called Oldani's in the Italian area of St. Louis known as The Hill. One of the restaurant's cooks, Fritz (history only gives us his first name), mistakenly deep-fried a batch of ravioli when he thought a pot of hot oil was water. A variation has him simply knocking the ravioli into the oil accidentally. No matter, the tale proves that, as was the case with the chimichanga, good things can happen when food falls into the fryer.

Fettuccine Alfredo: Finicky new mom

For a chef, there may be no greater indignity than an inability to get your spouse to eat your cooking. This was the ignominy that Alfredo di Lelio was facing circa 1914. Now, di Lelio, who ran a fine restaurant in Rome called Trattoria Alfredo, did have a major factor working against him. His wife, Ines, had just given birth to a baby and the whole affair had completely ruined her appetite.

"It was a hell of a life," di Lelio was once quoted as saying. "Work all day and rock the baby at night. I had to do something."

Desperate, he went with the most comforting dish he could imagine. It featured wide noodles smothered in a heap of Parmesan cheese and *lots* of butter. In particular, the copious amounts of thick butter—yes, this was before cholesterol concerns and the widespread use of defibrillators—was so rich and inviting that it restored Ines's taste for food and gave di Lelio a signature dish. (The cream version that Americans love would emerge in the United States many decades later.)

Fettuccine Alfredo may have remained a curious local dish, if not for a little Hollywood glitz and some good old-fashioned American media attention. In 1927 Douglas Fairbanks and Mary Pickford (the Brad and Angelina of their day) were on vacation in Rome when they happened upon di Lelio's little trattoria. A genial host, di Lelio whipped up his house special for the stars, who loved it.

How much did they love it?

The pair returned to the restaurant later in the trip and gave di Lelio a golden fork-and-spoon-set to toss his creation. One was engraved with Pickford's signature and the other with Fairbanks's and each had the inscription *To Alfredo—the king of the noodles*. Upon returning to Hollywood, Fairbanks and Pickford praised the food to their movie star crowd, gaining a fair bit of publicity for the pasta in the process. But it was another zealot for Alfredo's work, *Saturday Evening Post* food writer George Rector, who brought it to the American masses. He wrote in his *Post* column, "Alfredo doesn't make fettuccine. He doesn't cook fettuccine. He achieves it."

Despite all his achievements, di Lelio decided to hang up his utensils in 1943, selling the restaurant, his recipes, and even his guest signature books and photos of famous patrons. (He did keep his gold fork and spoon, though.) Di Lelio apparently grew frustrated with food shortages brought on by World War II. Nevertheless, his heart must have still been in his artery-clogging dish because in 1950, spurred by some backers, di Lelio agreed to come out of retirement, opening a new restaurant in another part of Rome.

Both di Lelio's old restaurant, situated near the famous Piazza Navona, and his new one, located near Emperor Augustus's mausoleum, confusingly used the name Alfredo. But does it matter? They each served (and continue to serve today) the delectable dish made from the original recipe. One British patron visiting war-torn Rome just after World War II put it best after having a mouthwatering plate of fettuccine Alfredo. Shocked by its quality and decadence, he asked his companion, "Look here, old chap, who has really won the war?"

Filet-O-Fish: Religious rules

Do you ever wonder why a burger joint like McDonald's went into the fish business? Credit goes to the good churchgoing folk of Ohio.

The Filet-O-Fish was the brainchild of one of the company's early franchisees, Lou Groen. In 1958, after working in his father-in-law's restaurant, the Cincinnati native decided he wanted to start his own establishment. He'd seen ads for two chains: one for McDonald's with its fifteen-cent hamburgers and the other for a company called Beverly

Osborne Chicken Delight. He told his wife that whichever they chose, the pair would be stuck eating a lot of that type of food. Groen then asked which one they should go for. She went with the burgers.

Although Groen would own forty-three McDonald's in the Northern Kentucky/Greater Cincinnati area by the end of his career, the early days were tough going. It was just Groen, his wife, and a guy named George cleaning, cooking, and serving at that first shop. When it came to sales, there was also one standout glitch: Those savory all-beef patties were surprisingly unpopular on Fridays. Sadly, they were only bringing in a minuscule seventy-five dollars each Friday. Groen needed to think of something fast.

In the days before market research, Groen had the bright idea to go to the closest restaurant doing excellent Friday business to figure out what he was missing. So he headed over to Frisch's, which was the local Big Boy chain, and spied on the customers. He immediately noticed a trend. Instead of burgers or steak or chicken, patrons were buying fish dishes.

He now understood the situation. His area of Cincinnati was about 87 percent Catholic and, along with abstaining from meat during the forty days of Lent, many devotees also avoided it on Fridays. Groen decided he needed a fish sandwich. He came up with a special batter and a tartar sauce condiment and went to the company's famed owner, Ray Kroc, to get sign-off on his new creation.

Proving that even visionaries strike out sometimes, Kroc wasn't sold. He told Groen he had a nonmeat idea of his own. He called it the Hula Burger, but there was nothing festive about it. The sandwich was simply a cold bun with a pineapple in the middle. Groen knew better than to argue with the boss. Still, he was able to get one concession.

"Ray said to me, 'Well, Lou, I'm going to put your fish sandwich on [a menu] for a Friday. But I'm going to put my special sandwich on too—whichever sells most, that's the one we'll go with,'" Groen told the *Cincinnati Enquirer* in 2007. "Friday came and the word came out. I won hands down. I sold 350 fish sandwiches that day. Ray never did tell me how his sandwich did."

Despite the victory, McDonald's forced some modifications to the newly dubbed Filet-O-Fish. The company wanted the sandwich to sell for twenty-five cents, but Groen's prototype, which featured halibut, was going to cost thirty cents to make. Four-and-a-half decades after the sandwich debuted in 1962 Groen still insisted that halibut was the way to go. Nevertheless, he agreed to switch to Atlantic cod. It was a move that turned out not to hurt business too much.

"My fish sandwich was the first addition ever to McDonald's original menu," he said. "It saved my franchise."

It also went on to be a popular choice for all types of patrons, including Jews and Muslims who face dietary restrictions of their own. Still, Catholics remain a key reason for its success. One survey found that even today 23 percent of Filet-O-Fish sandwiches are sold during Lent.

French Dip Sandwich: Extra sauce

Here's what we know about the French dip sandwich (besides it being an absolutely tasty gravy-soaked French-roll-and-meat mouthful): It was invented in Los Angeles during the first two decades of the twentieth century and no individual chef or restaurant owner takes any credit for coming up with the idea. After that, the truth behind the dish creator debate depends on whether you believe the proprietors of two different famed Los Angeles restaurants—Philippe The Original (formerly known as Philippe's) or Cole's.

Philippe's claim involves a few different stories. The restaurant's original owner, Philippe Mathieu, relayed the tale to the *Los Angeles Times* this way in 1951: "One day a customer saw some gravy in the bottom of a large pan of roast meat. He asked me if I would mind dipping one side of the French roll in that gravy. I did, and right away five or six others wanted the same." After quickly running out of gravy, he came ready the next day, but found that the high demand even outpaced the extra supply of juice that he had prepared. After that, the sandwich became a staple.

The restaurant's own website has a small twist on the story. It pinpoints the invention to a 1918 miscue on the part of Mathieu. "Mathieu inadvertently dropped the sliced French roll into the roasting pan filled with juice still hot from the oven," the website claims. "The patron, a policeman, would take the sandwich anyway and returned the next day with some friends asking for more dipped sandwiches."

A third explanation, courtesy of a 2008 *San Gabriel Tribune* article, suggests that Mathieu used the gravy to soften a stale roll after a fireman complained. (For some reason men in uniform figure prominently in these stories.)

Not to be outdone, Cole's has its own lore. According to its owners in a 2009 *Los Angeles Times* story, the dish was created in 1908 when a customer with sore gums requested the sandwich be dipped in the au jus to make it easier on his mouth.

Coming to a definitive answer on this one is unlikely. At one point a reporter from the *Los Angeles Business Journal* asked a city historian if he could shed light on the roots of the iconic local dish. The city employee's deadpan answer: "We don't have a French dip department."

Amazingly, both restaurants still exist more than a hundred years after they first opened. That said, they've both gone through changes with Philippe's shifting locations in the 1950s and Cole's closing down for a spell in 2007. As for which establishment serves the best French dip, that answer is as unclear as the sandwich's provenance (the traditional French dip is made with roast beef, though other meats like lamb and turkey are also used nowadays). Whatever the case, it seems that both restaurants are happy to simply stake their claim to the dish's origins and let the other do its business. Philippe's co-owner Richard Binder philosophically summed up the debate in 2009 by saying, "Who knows what happened a hundred years ago? We're just happy to still be around."

Philly Cheesesteak: Hungry hot dog vendor

In the early 1930s, the lives of Pat and Harry Olivieri were dominated by one thing: hot dogs. The brothers ran a South Philadelphia stall and worked hard slinging the popular fast food during these Depression years. With hot dogs weighing heavily on Pat's mind most of the time, it's not surprising that one day he wanted a change.

He sent off for a pound of steak (cost: seven cents) and decided that instead of tube meat he was going to rustle up something different on his hot dog griddle. He combined the meat, which was thinly sliced, with some cut onion and put them onto an Italian roll. This mouth-watering grease-fiesta of a sandwich wasn't meant for customers; Pat planned for it to be *his* own hot dog break.

Enter an unnamed cabbie who wouldn't take no for an answer. A popular spot for the working man, Pat and Harry's hot dog stand was a regular haunt for taxi drivers. One happened to come for a dog just when Pat was about to enjoy his diverting meal. The customer took one look at the sandwich—and, probably more importantly, smelled it—and told him to forget the hot dog. He wanted Pat's meal. A businessman first, Pat agreed to sell it for a dime.

And thus the basis for the Philly cheesesteak was born. In reality, it could have had a short life if not for the aforementioned cabbie, who was smitten by the new dish. He began telling his fellow hacks about it and before long they were lining up asking for the same sandwich. Pat and Harry were hot dog men, but they saw a great opportunity. So in came the new steak sandwich. The pair ultimately opened up Pat's King of Steaks not far from the original stall.

Over the years the sandwich has evolved. Cheese was added in the 1950s with Cheez Whiz becoming the preferred choice of purists (though I'm not sure you should use *purists* with any mention of Cheez Whiz). Provolone or American can be used, but you shouldn't stray too far from the basic cheese options. One-time presidential candidate John Kerry got grief for asking for swiss cheese. The request, along with Kerry's dainty style of eating the beast of a sandwich, led one local news-paperman to write that "the man who would be president of the people was photographed delicately grip-ping the sandwich with his finger-tips like he's some kind of Boston blue blood playing the piccolo."

Other popular additions include sautéed mushrooms with ketchup and sweet peppers some-times thrown in. There is even appropriate language: Customers are meant to ask for a sandwich "wit' or "wit out" various toppings.

Regrettably, these being the tough streets of South Philly, the complete story of the cheesesteak is not a fairy tale. By the 1950s, the Olivieris had heated competition from other steak sandwich estab-lishments. In 1966 Geno's Steaks set up shop right across the street. Geno's owner Joey Vento has long claimed his family first added the cheese to the cheesesteak, and the two shops have been in a heated—but good-natured—sandwich war since.

The battles don't stop there. In the 1970s, Pat left the business to move to Southern California. A legal tussle broke out between Pat's son and Harry's children over ownership of the now iconic spot (famed guests have included Presidents Bill Clinton and Barack Obama, and the restaurant had a cameo in the Oscar-winning movie *Rocky*). One of Harry's children, Frank, bought out the business, but a fight broke out again in 2006 when the current owner, Frank Jr., sued his cousin Rick (Pat's grandson), who was running a competing cheesesteak stand, for trademark infringement. At least it's the type of scrapping that would have made Rocky Balboa proud.

Sandwiches: Focused gambler

Time sure has a way of rehabilitating a reputation. Just ask the descendants of John Montagu, the fourth Earl of Sandwich. Born in 1718, the Earl of Sandwich took to politics at a young age and served in many high-profile roles in British government.

Alas, Sandwich's reputation during his lifetime—and for a very long time afterwards—was less than stellar. He was criticized for negotiating unfavorable terms when brokering the Treaty Aix-la-Chapelle, ending the War of Austrian Succession in 1748. Later the Earl was derided by the public for helping prosecute politician and journalist John Wilkes for writing a ribald poem.

And worst of all (from the British perspective), many have credited his performance as the first lord of admiralty during the American Revolution as a key reason the colonies won.

He was so bad, one British historian claimed, that during the Revolutionary War some officers refused commands rather than serve under Sandwich, who was said to have focused intently on patronage rather than ability when filling most positions.

"There may have been . . . worse administrators of the Navy; [but] there never was one who succeeded in attracting to himself such universal opprobrium," the historian explained in 1919. "He sold his country for parliamentary votes, and the weakness of our Navy in the American War was the result."

Now this line of history may be a bit overblown. After all, he did sponsor Captain James Cook's voyages and, if history had shifted a bit in his favor, we'd still be calling Hawaii by its original name—the Sandwich Islands—after the earl.

But what really saved Montagu from history's hall of shame was his penchant for gambling. The earl was well-known in his day as a libertine. Among his many vices, he had a longtime mistress with whom he had four children, and the man loved to drink. As one contemporary, Lord Chesterfield, put it, "He was a most profligate and abandoned character."

In 1762 the forty-four-year-old earl was also indulging in card playing. The story goes that during heated games, the earl refused to put down his cards and leave the table when it was time to eat. To solve the problem he insisted that typical fare such as roast beef and cheese be placed in between two pieces of bread so he could hold his cards with one hand and chow down with the other. A slight variation on this tale has Sandwich concerned that if he used his hands to pick up food, it would leave smudges and make it easier for his opponents to identify cards. (For those supporters of the earl, there is a benign but far less popular offering that had him toiling late into the night in front of papers, requiring a free hand to continue his work.)

The earl's creation was not the first filled-bread invention. Romans and early Jews, among others, were known for placing food in between bread products. But the Earl of Sandwich's notoriety at a time when the British Empire was vast meant that stories of his habit could travel worldwide and become the moniker for the dish.

For his descendants, this legacy has proved a lot easier to swallow than all the criticism. In 2001 the eleventh Earl of Sandwich and his son Orlando Montagu decided to cash in on the family name, opening up a chain of restaurants called the Earl of Sandwich.

Keeping with the lore of the fourth earl, all the establishment's sandwiches are made small enough to hold in one hand—even if patrons aren't playing card games or doing work. Fittingly, the restaurant chain has "The Original 1762," featuring hot roast beef, cheddar cheese, and horseradish sauce. There is also an "All American" sandwich on the menu, which considering the namesake's bad history with the former colonies, may want to be reconsidered.

Tempura: Missionaries' menu

The Japanese have brought a lot of fantastic things to this world: those slightly eerie, almost-human robots; sushi. . . . But amazingly, tempura, one of the country's best-known dishes, is not one of them. Tempura was initially introduced by Portuguese visitors, who saw it as nothing more than a way to help maintain their religious zeal while in a foreign land.

During the age of exploration, the Portuguese were among the most intrepid. On September 23, 1543, two Portuguese merchants first made contact with the Japanese, selling two guns to a feudal lord on the island of Tanegashima. Once trading opened up (the Japanese bartered for lots of Western products besides Portuguese guns), Catholic missionaries followed. They included St. Francis Xavier, who spent most of his life traveling abroad preaching.

These devout missionaries and merchants carefully followed all the Catholic holidays while spending time in Japan. A big one in the sixteenth century was Ember Days. During this event, which took place four times a year, Catholics were required to abstain from meat.

While the Portuguese were observant, it didn't mean they'd completely lost their appetite. Longing for some flavor from home, the foreigners cooked up some *yoshoku* (Western food). They breaded shrimp and fish and fried them with oil (likely sesame oil). Numerous scholars say that the word *tempura* came from part of the Latin for Ember Days—*quattour tempora*—with tempora, meaning "times," being the basis for naming this new style of cooking. Taking Western words and adding them to the Japanese lexicon was not uncommon during this era. Terms like *tabako* (tobacco), *pan* (bread), and *juban* (undershirt) all came from words brought to Japanese shores by foreigners.

Still, the batter-fried dish wasn't initially a hit amongst the Japanese. The Western version didn't sit well with locals because it was likely a lot heavier than the fluffy batter used today. Some suggest that the Portuguese recipe for tempura was more about oiling up food than adding a crispy exterior.

By the 1770s the Japanese had made changes to the process. The newer version had fish and vegetables wrapped in udon noodles. The lighter fare was skewered on bamboo sticks and became a popular choice at street stalls, where customers could eat it without the need of chopsticks.

Since then tempura has developed into one of the country's most recognizable dishes. The batter has become lighter over the years with egg, water, and flour as popular ingredients for breading everything from shellfish, octopus, and fish to all sorts of veggies. Nevertheless, the divine role played by Christian missionaries is not forgotten.

"I had long heard that the origin of tempura could be traced to Portuguese cooking, and imagined that those original squid fritters had simply been 'Japanized,'" wrote Takashi Morieda, an expert on Japanese cuisine. "But upon closer scrutiny, it becomes clear that what the Japanese actually acquired was an understanding of the deep-frying process—and from that point, tempura evolved to suit the country's own unique palate, thus integrating it into the heart of Japanese cuisine."

TV Dinners: Overstocked turkeys

When Gerry Thomas told listeners about how he created the TV dinner—those easily reheated, multipocket tin-tray meals—he gave the story a flair that only someone who knew how to sell could offer. Not surprisingly, Thomas was a salesman. In the early 1950s he made $200 a month for C. A. Swanson and Sons, which sold foodstuff in bulk to restaurants and other companies.

As Thomas relayed the tale, a business snafu provided him with the opportunity to change American eating habits. In the fall of 1951, abnormally temperate weather led to fewer turkeys being sold at Thanksgiving. "It was very warm on the East Coast, so there was less demand for turkeys," Thomas would recount more than fifty years later. This left Swanson with a staggering 520,000 pounds of surplus turkey meat. Without even a properly acclimatized warehouse to put the birds, the meat was stuck on refrigerated railway cars crisscrossing the United States.

Swanson needed a plan and Thomas stepped in. On a sales call in Pittsburgh, he came across a single-compartment metal tray that was being used by Pan Am Airlines for in-flight meals on overseas journeys. Thomas asked if he could have one of the trays and on the flight back to Swanson's Omaha, Nebraska, headquarters he took inspiration from his find and sketched a modified three-compartment tray. The final part of his plan came while walking by an appliance store. He saw a group huddled around the window, rubbernecking to check out a small 10-inch screen.

"I figured if you could borrow from that, maybe you could get some attention," Thomas said in a 1999 interview.

These trays—and his marketing plan—would be the answer to Swanson's turkey problem, he told his bosses. Along with turkey covered with gravy and a corn bread dressing, the original TV dinners included sweet potatoes and buttered peas. In 1953 they made their debut at ninety-eight cents a dinner and became an instant hit with approximately ten million units sold in the first year. According to Thomas, his reward was a salary increase to $300 a month and a $1,000 bonus.

This story has been endorsed in one form or another by many people. The Frozen Food Hall of Fame inducted Thomas into its ranks for his work on the TV dinner. In 1999 he had his hands (and a tray) immortalized in cement outside Hollywood's famous Chinese Theatre. Even *Maxim* magazine ranked Thomas twenty-eighth on its list of the "50 Greatest Guys of the Century"—three spots ahead of James Bond, no less. In his later years, Thomas, who died in 2005, served as an ambassador for the dinner, traveling around with silver cufflinks in the shape of TV dinner trays (the Swanson family no longer owned the company by that point).

But with slick salesmen you have to be a little careful about what you're purchasing. Journalist Roy Rivenburg raised a number of questions about Thomas's story in a 2003 *Los Angeles Times* article. Rivenburg pointed out that rather than being unseasonably warm, November 1951 was unusually cold, throwing some doubt into the underpinning of the railway car story. Thomas would recant a bit on that fact, saying that the train story was "a metaphor" for an "annual problem" Swanson had when it came to unloading excess turkey meat. Rivenburg also offered alternative candidates as the TV dinner's true parents, including company heads Clarke and Gilbert Swanson and a handful of other employees at the company. Finally, he pointed out that other companies were selling similar types of frozen dinners before the TV dinner, suggesting that even if Thomas's inspiration was legit, he wasn't the first.

Still, nothing is definitive and Rivenburg did interview one figure knowledgeable about the origins of the trays who seemed to corroborate at least part of Thomas's claims. One thing is certain: Thomas's account was used for years as part of the TV dinner's marketing strategy with the media. Beyond that, it's buyer beware.

Desserts

Chocolate Chip Cookies: Missing ingredient

If you read the writings of Ruth Graves Wakefield, you'd think she was straight out of central casting for the domesticated housewife. She literally studied household arts at the Framingham State Normal School (class of 1924) and wrote cookbooks that encouraged new brides to "try a lot of these recipes, especially those which are your husband's favorites." She even laid out a list of thirty-six must-dos that every woman should perform in order to reach "your goal of being a proficient wife and hostess." (Example: serving perfect coffee.)

With words like that, you can just picture the perfectly dressed Mrs. Wakefield (apron nicely tied), serving a batch of her most famous creation: the chocolate chip cookie. She was surely a product of her times—for example, she would insist that there were "*no substitutes* [her italics] for butter [and] cream." But to put her in a box based on her writing isn't fair. In actuality, Wakefield was a successful writer, dietitian, lecturer, and businesswoman. And, as the regularly retold story goes, besides inventing the chocolate chip cookie to overcome a cooking problem she faced in the kitchen, she also knew how to capitalize on her unplanned discovery.

In August 1930, Ruth and her husband, Kenneth, purchased a Cape Cod–style house on the outskirts of Whitman, Massachusetts. The building was loaded with history. Erected in 1709, it had been used as a toll house and rest stop on the road between New Bedford and Boston. Drawing from history, the Wakefields turned the cozy spot into an inn, which they called The Toll House.

Considering her mastery of the household arts, Ruth probably ran many of the day-to-day elements of the hotel, but she was without a doubt queen of the kitchen. First published in 1936, her cookbook *Ruth Wakefield's Toll House Tried and True Recipes* went through some thirty-nine editions. It offers a spectrum of recipes for such tantalizing fare as onion soup, lobster thermidor, and chicken soufflé.

But it's her Toll House Chocolate Crunch Cookies that she became most known for. Amazingly this recipe, which calls for two bars of "Nestlé's yellow label chocolate, semi-sweet, which has been cut in pieces the size of a pea" was the first ever to include chocolate chips. That's saying a lot because cookies, which come from the Dutch word *koekje* (meaning "little cake"), have a history dating back to the seventh century and chocolate bars were invented in the mid-nineteenth century.

Why did Wakefield decide to change the destiny of the cookie? The vastly popular lore goes like this: In 1930 Wakefield was making butter cookies when she realized a key ingredient was missing (some say it was nuts, while others claim it was cooking chocolate). Either she didn't have the time or the inclination to pop out for the missing materials so she broke up some Nestlé chocolate bars with an ice pick and used those pieces instead. Much to her surprise the combination was fantastic and she christened her find Chocolate Crispies. Another slightly simpler version states that Wakefield simply threw chocolate pieces into cookie dough on a whim, stumbling into pure cookie heaven.

Nestlé discovered Wakefield's work when one of its salesmen began inquiring into why their chocolate bars were selling so well in Wakefield's town of Whitman. In 1939, Wakefield negotiated a forty-year contract with the company. That year Nestlé started selling their chocolate in "morsel" form—or as we better know them, as chips. They also printed Wakefield's recipe on the bag and renamed the confection Toll House Cookies.

Nestlé must have liked this tale because during the cookie's fiftieth anniversary proceedings in 1980, the accidental discovery story was offered up (those stories were running in newspapers by at least 1955). That said, a *Christian Science Monitor* article that ran in 1977, the year Wakefield died, asserted that Wakefield may have been more deliberate in her efforts. According to journalist Phyllis Hanes, who reported from Whitman, Wakefield had remembered experiments from her college food chemistry classes and resolved to come up with a new treat as an alternative to her crisp pecan icebox cookies. After trial-and-error, she and her pastry cook, Sue Bridges, developed the perfect recipe. Wakefield's own words seem to bolster this account. She once wrote, "Certainty in place of guessing eliminates failures." This suggests she wasn't one to haphazardly throw ingredients in a bowl and go for it.

If the *Monitor*'s story is accurate, Wakefield certainly showed a businesswoman's smarts. It appears she never publicly contradicted the more fanciful yarn—a shrewd choice that likely sold more bags of chocolate chips for Nestlé.

Chocolate Molten Cake (Chocolate Lava Cake): Celebrity chef flub

Even celebrity chefs get it wrong sometimes.

French native Jean-Georges Vongerichten made a name for himself in the ever-competitive New York City cooking scene and went on to establish restaurants throughout the world, including spots in such far-flung locales as the Bahamas and Shanghai. Though some have criticized the chef for spreading himself a bit too thin over the years, he is beloved by many discerning food critics.

One once wrote that "as gracefully as any of his peers, Jean-Georges Vongerichten shows that today's globe-trotting genre-straddling, hyperextended super chef can still create memorable—even riveting— meals." Another critic called him a "legend . . . one of the most influential and creative chefs of our time. His food, which eschews thick butter and cream sauces for vegetable broths, fruit juices, and infused oils, is extolled as being ethereally light, clean, and simple."

Yet back in 1987, he was a young chef with a lot on his mind. He was running the kitchen at the Restaurant Lafayette, located in Manhattan's now-defunct Drake Hotel. One night Vongerichten was charged with putting together a private dinner for 300 guests. It was a tall task for a man who at the time hadn't experienced the crush of cooking so many dishes for a group. This was particularly the case when it came to preparing a slew of the small chocolate cakes that were set for the evening's menu.

"Baking one and baking 300 is different," he told the *Chicago Tribune* in 2006. "They were supposed to be cooked through, but the oven temperature dropped. We miscalculated the timing." The result was a cake that had a firm outer shell and a chocolate gooey center. Before he realized the miscue, the cakes were in the dining room. Vongerichten claimed that not only were people chowing down, but they were also "screaming wanting the recipe."

He would go on to name the dish Valrhona cake with vanilla ice cream (Valrhona is the name of the chocolate he used in making the dessert). The rest of America embraced it as chocolate molten cake or chocolate lava cake (my family simply calls it "the ooze"). Others—particularly some French pastry chefs—have claimed to be the first, but Vongerichten brought celebrity to the dish. As Jacques Torres, a longtime pastry chef at iconic New York establishment Le Cirque, put it, "He was the first to make it in America, but it existed in France already."

Interestingly, Vongerichten did not always tell such a colorful origin story. In 1991, just a few years after he introduced his creation, the chef told prominent *New York Times* food writer Florence Fabricant that he got the recipe for the cake from his mother. At the time a number of other ambitious chefs were trying to stake a claim to the cake's provenance so maybe Vongerichten felt he needed a more iron-clad story. As he got older, perhaps he felt more confident to disclose the truth behind the sweet dish. Whatever the case, the undercooked cake tale has become part of his lore and his dessert has developed into a staple at high-end dining spots as well as places that Jean-Georges might not approve of.

Cookies 'n Cream Ice Cream: Short work break

John Harrison may very well have the greatest job on the planet. As the official taste tester for Edy's Grand Ice Cream, he spends all day making sure various flavors meet quality control standards. He even uses a gold spoon, as wood and plastic varieties leave an aftertaste and silver tends to tarnish. All told, he's checked approximately 200 million gallons of the sweet delicacy—though his doctor would be happy to know that he doesn't swallow any of the scoops he samples. As he puts it, he has a three-step process: "Swirl, smack, and spit . . . You're going to get the appearance, you're going to get the flavor, and you're going to get the texture. And that's what you're looking for." Along with tasting, Harrison, a fourth generation ice-cream man, also dabbles in creation, having developed more than seventy new flavors.

Yet his biggest discovery—Cookies 'n Cream—didn't come from advanced testing, but from a need to snack quickly before getting back on the job. In 1982, while taking a break from the lab (yep, ice-cream tasters have a laboratory), he wanted a simple scoop of vanilla, which is Harrison's favorite. He went to the company ice-cream parlor and alongside his bowl were a few chocolate cookies. Ironically, he didn't have a lot of time to eat his ice cream because he needed to get back to tasting ice cream. To speed up the process, he broke up the cookies and tossed them in with his snack. Harrison, who reportedly has his nine thousand taste buds insured for one million dollars, immediately knew he was savoring something special.

"I was in a hurry," said Harrison reflecting on the moment nearly two decades later in a 2001 *Reading Eagle* article. "And I thought it would just be faster if I put the cookies into the ice cream. Cookies 'n Cream was invented by accident."

As simple as the cookies-plus-vanilla-ice-cream-combo might seem, nobody had mass-produced the product. At least two others in the 1970s—a South Dakota State University dairy plant manager named Shirley W. Seas and Massachusetts ice-cream parlor owner Steve Herrell—have claimed to have been first with the idea. But nothing had hit the worldwide market until Harrison threw together the mixture.

Interestingly, it required an act of God for Edy's to jump on the opportunity to sell the stuff. When Harrison went to his bosses with his new flavor, they originally weren't too interested. They believed it was too much of a kids' flavor and worried it wouldn't have mass appeal. Luckily for Cookies 'n Cream lovers everywhere, the winter of 1982 didn't treat peaches in the South very kindly. Huge hail storms decimated the crop, which left Edy's in a dilemma. They'd planned on rolling out a Perfectly Peach flavor, but they weren't going to have enough fruit to make it happen.

Harrison stepped up, going back into the file cabinet and suggesting that the company use his cookie-and-cream ice-cream concoction as a replacement. The company, which is also known as Dreyer's in the western United States, agreed but did so reluctantly. In 1983 executives said they'd give the flavor ninety days and then reassess. Within no time, Cookies 'n Cream was a hit, becoming the fifth-highest selling flavor in the word—a lofty height that Perfectly Peach would have probably never reached.

Crêpes Suzette: Clumsy waiter

Henri Charpentier was a true bon vivant. A chef of the highest order, he worked at top-notch restaurants in Paris as well as the Savoy in London before being lured to the United States to run the kitchen at New York's famed Delmonico's. A storyteller with a knack for drama, he once declared he made four million dollars as a chef and restaurateur before losing it all. That would be an impressive feat for a man whose career primarily spanned the first half of the twentieth century.

Yet for all his success (and failure), Charpentier's greatest claim to history occurred when he was a clumsy sixteen-year-old boy.

I would not do his tale justice, so I now hand it over to Charpentier, who explained just months before he died how he allegedly created crêpes Suzette in Monte Carlo in 1896:

> I was only sixteen and serving the Prince of Wales, son of Queen Victoria, later King Edward VIII of England. Among the diners at the Prince's table was a beautiful French girl named Suzette. I cannot recall her last name. It does not matter.
>
> His highness ordered crêpes—the French pancakes. I mixed the sauce, and added a brandy blend of my own. As I did, the heat of the chafing dish accidentally set the simmering cordials afire.

I was embarrassed but I did not show it. I poured the fiery sauce on the crêpes, as if the flames were set on purpose. The prince tasted. Then he smiled and said: "Henri, what have you done with these crêpes? They are superb."

I was thrilled and offered to name them in his honor. But he declined. "Henri," he said, "we must always remember that the ladies come first. We will call this glorious thing crêpes Suzette." That was the day, monsieur. People had been eating pancakes from the days of Napoleon—even the Romans—but never before that day crêpes Suzette.

According to Charpentier's 1934 autobiography, *Life à la Henri*, the Prince sent over "a jeweled ring, a Panama hat, and a cane" the next day in gratitude for his creation.

There are numerous experts who question this story. *The Oxford Companion to Food* insists it was developed at Paris's Restaurant Paillard in 1889 and named after an actress who played a chambermaid serving pancakes in a contemporary comedy. The food encyclopedia does point out that this original version did not have liquor and was not flamed at the table like Charpentier's bungled effort.

However preposterous, it's hard not to root for the veracity of Charpentier's story. Late in life, he found himself in the Southern California seaside town of Redondo Beach financially broken with just ten dollars in his pocket. He secured a very small space—described once as "unglamorous as a hamburger stand"—and began serving a single dinner to one party a night. Groups of between twelve and sixteen guests would beg to score a table and indulge in the master's cooking, for which he charged an extremely reasonable eight dollars a head. His patrons had to be incredibly patient: It took *four years* to get in for a meal.

Charpentier, who passed away in 1961, could have cashed in on his notoriety, but he seemed pleased to take things slow. "I only make enough money to live. . . . My reward is the joy of good eating, good companionship, and happy diners," he said.

His crêpes Suzette story is likely a tall tale, but if that's the only reason he's remembered today, I'm buying.

Granny Smith Apples: Garbage discovery

Quick quiz: Which of the following was an actual person: Betty Crocker, Granny Smith, or Aunt Jemima? As we're talking about those great green apples in this section (America's favorite apple pie filler), I'm sure you're not surprised that the correct answer is Granny Smith. Before she was a granny, Maria Smith had lived a lot of life. Born in 1800 in Sussex, England, Maria, along with her husband, Thomas, and their five children, emigrated to New South Wales, Australia, in 1838. After a number of years in the new country, the family bought a thirty-four-acre farm for £605 (approximately $56,000 in today's dollars) and started growing fruit.

Although the Smiths were producing a number of fruits, the famed apples that bear Maria's name weren't a part of the crop. Truth be told, with five children and, by that time, grandchildren (hence the granny sobriquet), Mrs. Smith probably wasn't intently focused on picking or growing in the farm's early years. But by the late 1860s, Thomas had become infirm, forcing the aging grandmother to take over the business.

It was during this period that Maria made her discovery, which was, without a doubt, never planned. Smith's grandson Benjamin Spurway recounted years later that Smith had been given French crab apples from Tasmania by a fruit agent and Granny used them to produce apple pies. She discarded the unused peels and cores through an open window next to the kitchen. Sometime later she noticed a seedling growing near her wall with an odd new apple. Another variation on the story has Granny dumping rotting French crabs beside a nearby creek and discovering a wee new apple tree there.

In either case, this type of serendipitous creation through open pollination isn't incredibly uncommon. Still, it rarely produces such a perfect fruit. (The dual purpose Granny Smith apple is great for both cooking and eating raw.) The beauty of the new apple wasn't immediately identified by all. When she showed some to neighbors in 1868, the apples received little fanfare. Granny died in 1870, but her apples continued on as members of her family began cultivating the new variety. In 1890 they were exhibited at the Castle Hill Agricultural and Horticultural Show. The next year they won top prize for cooking apples at the event.

Granny Smith apples really gained attention after World War I when Australian industry looked to mass ship its produce abroad. They became popular in the United States in the 1960s and by 1975 Granny Smiths represented 50 percent of all Australian apple exports (and 40 percent of the country's overall crop). They are also produced in such Southern Hemisphere locales as New Zealand, Chile, Argentina, and South Africa. The reason for their popularity? Along with boasting excellent acidity and texture when stewed and offering a good combination of sweet and tart, Granny Smith apples also have another key characteristic—they're tough. The apple remains edible after up to six months in cold storage and it "is nearly as resilient as a tennis ball and holds up well in shipping," according to food author Roger Yepsen.

It seems appropriate that the apple that bears Maria Smith's name would be as hardy as the woman who moved from one side of the world to the other, raised five children, tended to an invalid husband, and ran a farm.

Rhubarb: Bumbling builders

Rhubarb, when combined with strawberries, makes such a perfect crumble or pie that it's often known in foodie circles as "pie plant." In fact, although rhubarb is a vegetable, the US customs court in Buffalo, New York, broke with reality—and the fact that it's often used in savory sauces—and decreed it a fruit in 1947 because it was so popular as a dessert stuffing. But it wasn't always like that. Without a construction mistake, rhubarb might have never truly developed into a good go-to dessert option.

Humans have been aware of rhubarb for more than two thousand years (some suggest even longer than that). In the wild, it's common in cool climates. Gatherers in places like Mongolia and Siberia were the first to pull its roots. While some stout Siberians stuck the veggie in pies, most people recoiled at adding early rhubarb to a regular diet. The celery-looking stalks were extremely acidic and not too pleasing to the palate.

Instead, rhubarb was used for medicinal purposes. Though it can be toxic if you take too much of it (chomping on the leaves can make you really sick), the veggie is full of oxalic acid. Today oxalic acid is used in cleaning supplies, but the ancient Greeks, Romans, and Chinese, and even the more modern British thought it was helpful for such maladies as a persistent cough. Henry VIII supposedly used rhubarb-based medicine for a long stretch late in his life. In the seventeenth century, its dried root was so coveted in England that it cost three times the price of opium. Despite the high street value, I somehow have a hard time seeing rhubarb pushers sneaking around back alleys.

As a cherished commodity, rhubarb was grown in a small plot at the posh Chelsea Physic Garden in London. Nevertheless, it must not have been too much of a focus because when some workers were brought to the garden to dig a trench near the rhubarb patch in 1815, they didn't give the vegetable any thought. Rather than dumping the spoil from the ditch into an unused area, they tossed the dirt right on top of the garden's rhubarb crowns.

The rhubarb was then forgotten until it was time to fill the trench again (what work was being done isn't known). Once the spoil was cleared, the garden's curator William Anderson made an unexpected discovery. Instead of the normal cherry-red-stalked rhubarb, up popped a paler, more tender variation of the vegetable. Anderson must have taken a taste and found the flavor to be far mellower than rhubarb's normal eye-watering tang. He started testing the discovery and in 1816 sent off his findings to the Royal Horticulture Society. It turned out that when rhubarb was packed in extra soil (and fortified with manure) it thrived. Special pots were created to help the process.

An area of Yorkshire in northern England—dubbed "the rhubarb triangle"—developed into the center of its cultivation. Over time, those exacting gardeners up north learned that a little additional luck probably further aided the London discovery of the far more edible rhubarb. It turns out that not only is a load of dirt needed for what is now known as forced growth rhubarb, but temperatures also have to be just right (approximately 55°F to 65°F). Though the weather can be notoriously temperamental in London, it must have stayed just constant enough at the Chelsea Physic Garden following the worker's flub to ensure that we have the finest rhubarb-strawberry pies today.

Tarte Tatin: Ditzy sister

The history of the popular French dessert tarte Tatin is a tale of two sisters. In 1888, Stephanie and Caroline Tatin inherited the Hotel Tatin from their father. Located in the Loire Valley in the small town of Lamotte-Beuvron, the hotel, which also featured a restaurant, was a success under the sisters' stewardship.

There were two key reasons why it thrived. The first was the bounce the hotel received from Napoleon III. The monarch owned an estate not far from the hotel and stocked the area with game. As a result, hunters flocked to this part of the Sologne region. With the hotel strategically located across the street from the train station, it picked up tons of patrons. The second reason was Stephanie was a really good cook. While the younger Caroline—nicknamed "the little princess of Sologne"—was a socially adept hostess, the older Stephanie showed exceptional talent in the kitchen, while also having a reputation as somewhat of an airhead.

It was the combination of these factors that many claim led to the invention of the tarte Tatin. One day during the height of the hunting season in the 1890s, the hotel's restaurant was incredibly crowded. Stephanie was trying to keep up with demand, but the scatterbrained chef neglected a pan full of apples she'd left simmering in butter over a fire. Alternatively, some believe that she had planned to line the pan with pastry dough before putting the apples on but neglected to do so in her rush. Whatever the case, many cooks might have been unsure about what to do with the seemingly wasted apples, but proving her space cadet reputation may have been a bit unwarranted, Stephanie improvised by putting a pastry shell over the now caramelized fruits and shoving the combination into the oven. When it finished baking, she turned the pie upside down and, voilà, the tarte Tatin was born.

Serious foodies hate this story. Many have pointed out that similar tarts—some with apples and others with pears—were popular in the Sologne region before Stephanie's supposed mistake. One particularly inspired Tatin-ologist has argued that a chef from the estate of a local count was the actual inventor of the dessert. This claim suggests that the Tatin family was given the recipe details and Stephanie simply followed the directions. But nothing has been proved conclusively and, as Florence Fabricant pointed out in *The New York Times Dessert*

Cookbook, the tarte Tatin—probably thanks in part to the fun accident story—has received "excellent PR" over the years.

By the 1920s word of the invention story and the fantastic new recipe had reached Paris. Maurice-Edmond Sailland, who was known by his pen name Curnonsky and was considered the "Prince of Gastronomy," discovered the tarte Tatin and included it in his influential survey of French cuisine, *La France Gastronomique*. The famed Parisian restaurant Maxim's would soon include the dessert on its menu, leading to another popular (though likely apocryphal) tale that the happening Paris hot spot sent a spy posing as a gardener to the Tatins' restaurant to snatch the recipe.

Neither Stephanie, who passed away in 1917, nor Caroline, who died in 1911, was alive to see their confectionary namesake make it to the big time. The sisters never even called the dish the tarte Tatin and reportedly never wrote down the recipe. Accident or not, the caramelized, buttery treat was proudly prepared for all the patrons who came to their hotel. The restaurant, which still exists today, continues to have one rule about the dessert: It has to be served hot out of the oven.

Candies and Snacks

Cheese Puffs: Rabbit food

Junk food haters who say cheese puffs—aka cheese curls—aren't fit for human consumption may be unconsciously referring to the product's origin. Best known by such brand names as Cheetos and Cheez Doodles, this powdered mess of a snack got its start from a machine that manufactured food for animals.

In the 1930s the Flakall Company based in Beloit, Wisconsin, ran a successful business creating corn-based livestock feed. The company's machine was particularly useful because it broke down dangerously sharp corn hulls by flaking the grain into easily digestible small pieces. The feed became popular, particularly for rabbits, who were the first to indulge in the mashed-up food. With demand high, the equipment, known as an extruder, would often run continuously. This was an intense process and parts could get extremely hot during the flaking procedure. To solve the problem, workers would pour moistened corn kernels into the extruder to cool things down and ease clogging.

One day a Flakall employee (most say his name was Edward Wilson) noticed an interesting by-product from the cooling efforts. The moistened kernels were turning into long white ribbons of cornmeal as they moved through the machine. Once these strips exited, they would harden and become puffy. Wilson was intrigued by this unintended creation and took home a bag of the fluff. There, his wife fried up the puffs, added a dash of salt, and shared them with neighbors. This being Wisconsin, the locals asked that a little cheese be added to the mix. The snack was dubbed the Korn Kurl.

In 1942 Flakall secured a patent for a machine dedicated to churning out these corn puffs. Undoubtedly recognizing the contraption's animal-food roots, the instrument's inventors made sure to point out in their patent application that "[w]hen streamlets are discharged from the processing apparatus they are prepared for human consumption." The machine was good to go, but hungry mobs outside of Beloit would have to wait to get their cheese puff fix. During World War II, the government put a halt to the production of any nonessential food. Somehow, the Korn Kurl fell into that category (partying teenagers, if they'd known about the product, would have let out a collective groan at that decision).

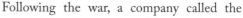

Following the war, a company called the Adams Corporation became the first to use the machine for commercial use. Not long after, in 1948, the San Antonio–based Frito Company introduced Cheetos nationally. And in the 1950s, a New York–based company, called Old London Foods, began marketing Cheez Doodles, reaching stores across the country by the mid-1960s.

The snack has flown off convenience store shelves ever since. Cheetos alone produce four billion dollars in annual sales worldwide and, if you were to put the yearly output of Cheez Doodles end-to-end on the ground, it would span approximately seventy-two miles. Moreover, even with its beastly beginnings, the cheese puff has appealed to the more refined palate. Proving that point, Cheez Doodle inventor Morrie Yohai took great pride in one particular possession: a photo of gourmet TV personality Julia Child with her hand deep in a bag of Cheez Doodles.

Chewing Gum: Deposed dictator and a nosy accountant

If you think gnawing on a hard piece of gum must be the equivalent of chewing on a rubber tire, there's a reason for that. Americans can attribute the invention of the jaw chomping diversion to a man who initially thought gum would be great as a rubber substitute.

The basis for the first chewing gum was a substance known as chicle. A milky sap taken from the Mexican sapodilla tree, the substance made its way to the United States in a most unexpected way from a famously dubious character.

Antonio López de Santa Anna is best known as the Mexican general and politician responsible for the massacre at the Alamo. With Texas settlers trying to secede from Mexico, Santa Anna commanded his army to lay siege to the Alamo, ultimately slaughtering those defending the fort, including such notables as Jim Bowie and Davy Crockett. The Texans would eventually prevail against Santa Anna. While many of the Mexican leaders involved were executed for their part, Santa Anna was allowed to immigrate to America where he moved to Staten Island in New York (now that's a change of scenery!).

Not long after settling in, Santa Anna met an inventor named Thomas Adams, who observed how the former Mexican power broker liked to chew on these small pieces of chicle. Adams didn't really see the value in that. In the United States at the time, paraffin wax was the chew of choice. Instead, Adams sent away for a crate of chicle with a different goal in mind. He thought that with the right combination of chemicals Santa Anna's gummy substance could be transformed into a synthetic rubber. Adams failed in that endeavor, but between the former dictator's chewing and Adams' own son Horatio supposedly picking up the habit, he relented and began marketing his supply of chicle in 1871 as unwrapped balls. He called his creation "Adams New York Gum—Snapping and Stretching."

Chicle-based chewing gum became established by the start of the twentieth century, but it stretched to another level in 1928 when an unlikely source mistakenly created bubble gum. That individual was Walter Diemer and he wasn't an inventor like Thomas Adams or even a scientist. He was an accountant. Nevertheless he was an accountant at the right place for this sort of creation. He worked at the Fleer Chewing Gum Corporation and after being asked one day to keep an eye on some gum manufacturing while a colleague had to answer the phone, he became intrigued by the business. He developed such an interest that during down time he'd mess around with some of the product. This odd decision by the accountant shouldn't be too much of a surprise as Diemer was somewhat eccentric. Late in life he was known to ride around Lancaster, Pennsylvania, on a large-scale tricycle.

With no formal background, Diemer threw all sorts of things in his batches of gum. The company had previously made gum supple enough to blow bubbles, but the problem was the chewy substance would either be too sticky or would break apart. The cliché goes if you put a thousand monkeys in a room with typewriters and give them enough time they'll produce the great American novel. It seems that it only took one accountant and a handful of months to produce just the right bubble blowing consistency. His secret: latex. "It was an accident," Diemer told the *Lancaster (Pennsylvania) Intelligencer Journal* in 1996. "I was doing something else and ended up with something with bubbles."

After whipping up a batch, he decided he wanted to add a little color. For whatever reason, the only food coloring the Fleer plant had in stock was pink. For that fact alone, pink became the iconic color of bubble gum.

Fleer dubbed it Dubble Bubble and in the first year on the market it did $1.5 million in sales, surpassing the Tootsie Roll as the most popular one-cent candy. To this day, chewing gum has not lost its flavor:

Americans spend some $2.5 billion on about a half-billion pounds of gum every year. And, in sweet vindication for Thomas Adams, many modern gums use synthetic polymers like styrene-butadiene rubber, which is also in—you guessed it—car tires.

Doughnuts: Seafaring captain

It should come as no surprise that more than one person has taken credit for the design of the modern doughnut. After all, who wouldn't want to be responsible for such a satisfying treat? To quote the always sage Homer Simpson (who does not stake a claim): "Doughnuts. Is there anything they *can't* do?"

These fried cakes were first produced in sixteenth-century Holland and were called *olykoek* (translation: "oil cake"). They were made of sweetened dough and sometimes sugared. Early American connoisseurs of olykoek included Dutch settlers in New York and, despite their austere lifestyle, the Pilgrims in New England. They called the treats "dough nuts" because they were originally small—some were even walnut-size.

The big breakthrough came with the invention of the hole in the middle. The problem with the old school version of the pastry was that it would not fry uniformly and, inevitably, the center of the treat would become soggy with excess oil. With a hole in the center, surface area increased and the doughnut became all the more perfect.

So who was the genius who invented nothing? This important question was one that required serious debate. In 1941 the Doughnut

Corporation of America set up a confab at the swanky Astor Hotel in New York City to address this very issue. The company convened a three-person panel of celebrity judges: quiz show host Clifton Fadiman, journalist Franklin Adams, and gossip columnist/professional hostess Elsa Maxwell. Their job was to determine the following, "Who put the hole in the doughnut?"

While at least one food historian gives the honor to the Pennsylvania Dutch (they wanted to make dunking their doughnuts in coffee easier), the two contenders for the crown at this debate relied on either a fortuitous accident or some improvised inspiration.

The first contestant was an unnamed Native American from Cape Cod. Henry A. Ellis, a lawyer from the Cape, is generally credited as the man making the argument on behalf of the anonymous member of the Nauset tribe. Ellis claimed that the brave in question shot an arrow straight through the middle of a Pilgrim's fry cake creating the first holed doughnut. Despite his courtroom background, Ellis's argument wasn't much of one. He lacked any tangible evidence to back up his story.

His opponent, Fred Crockett, was better prepared. Crockett entered the fray on behalf of his cousin Hanson Crockett Gregory, bearing letters and affidavits to support his case. Crockett said that in 1847, a teenage Gregory, who would go on to become a renowned ship captain in Maine, heard his mom complaining that the centers of her doughnuts were getting too soggy. The brash young man got up, walked across the room, and stuck his fork through the center of one of the cakes—problem solved.

Crockett won the day with that simple explanation. It was enough for the town of Camden, Maine, to erect a plaque in Gregory's honor in 1947 calling him "The Inventor of the Hole in the Doughnut." Despite Crockett's victorious account, others have told Gregory's story differently. The most fanciful version features sea captain Gregory fighting a terrible storm and needing somewhere to put his doughnut. With little choice, he stuck it on a spoke of his ship's wheel, creating the hole. In her comprehensive volume, *The Donut Book: The Whole Story in Words, Pictures & Outrageous Tales*, Sally Levitt Steinberg persuasively argues that the popular ship's wheel anecdote came from a children's book fictionalizing Gregory's discovery called *Cap'n Dow and the Hole in the Doughnut*.

As for Gregory himself, he also weighed in on the topic. During an interview at the dawn of the twentieth century, Gregory told a reporter for the *Boston Post* he'd grown sick of eating tough doughnuts known as "greasy sinkers." Considering his frustration briefly, he took off the ship's tin pepper box and cut into the middle of the cake. It was, he said, "the first hole ever seen by mortal eyes." Reflecting on his offhanded discovery, he added, "Of course, a hole ain't so much, but it's the best part of the doughnut—you'd think so if you had ever tasted the doughnuts we used to eat." Homer Simpson would unquestionably agree.

Graham Crackers: Sex-ruining snack

Graham crackers will wreck your sex life. At least that's what their creator, Sylvester Graham, hoped.

In the early 1800s Graham, a trained preacher and self-styled medical guru, was very concerned about people's sex life—or as he called it "venereal excess." He was convinced that getting down (in a biblical sense) caused such physical maladies as headaches, poor circulation, epilepsy, and even spinal disease. No offense to the good reverend, but I have to wonder if he was doing it right.

Graham believed that what you ate was at the root of sexual desire, which included masturbation—an act he was particularly jittery about. He said: "high-seasoned food; rich dishes; the free use of flesh . . . all, more or less—and some to a very great degree—increase the concupiscent excitability and sensibility of the genital passions." As a result, Graham, who started the American Vegetarian Society, insisted that meat, oils, alcohol, sugar, fats, and refined white flour all be cut from diets.

Lest you think that Graham was off-kilter, he attracted a pretty huge following in the late 1820s and into the 1830s. He  set up boarding houses in New York and Boston for people who wanted to follow the path of temperance and abstinence and even had devotees on college campuses. The folks at Oberlin College, for example, "enthusiastically embraced" Graham's principles. His adherents even had a name: Grahamites.

This isn't to say the man didn't have detractors. Along with his ascetic ways, Graham was considered aloof and cranky by many (wouldn't you be?). He was apparently attacked by mobs on at least three occasions, including one group of butchers and bakers who believed Graham was running them out of business. Famed writer Ralph Waldo Emerson contemptuously called him the "poet of bran."

What we think of today as a great kids' treat was devised by the reverend in 1829 as part of his clean living regime. His crackers were made with unsifted wheat flour. It was less processed than other crackers on the market and Graham hoped it, along with similarly made "Graham bread," would serve as a vital foundation for suppressing lustful urges.

By the end of the 1830s, Graham had lost his following. And despite his healthy ways, he died in 1851 at age fifty-seven. Still, a number of his teachings, like regularly brushing teeth—something that wasn't common back then—and taking regular showers are the norm nowadays.

As for his crackers, modern varieties typically have sugar in them and are made with refined flour (the horror!). Ironically, today's starchy graham crackers can stick to teeth and wreak havoc on oral hygiene. If that wasn't bad enough, what Graham would have thought of the devilish combination of his eponymous crackers with marshmallows and chocolate—aka s'mores—one can only imagine.

Jelly Tots: Camera-ready treat

Americans might not know much about Jelly Tots, but if you're British, South African, or Canadian, these soft sugarcoated gumdrops were likely an indispensable item in your childhood diet. The nostalgia for these candies can run deep. Case in point: In 2010 a woman from Manchester, England, changed her name from Jane Nash to "Miss Jelly St Tots" for her fortieth birthday in honor of the confection. It's unclear whether Miss Jelly St Tots would have such devotion if she knew that the first Jelly Tots came close to being thrown in the garbage before anyone even took a taste.

Brian Boffey was a research scientist for the famed north England candy maker, Rowntrees, when he inadvertently made the first batch of tots in the late 1960s. He had been working on creating a powdered jelly that would set immediately when hitting cold water. (Think Jell-O mix that could be ready as soon as water was added.) It was a quixotic endeavor that would never successfully be completed.

But his failure didn't come from a lack of effort. He tried just about everything, even running high-speed photography experiments to figure out how drops of gelatin were formed. During his photo shoot, some of those gelatinous bits landed on a sugar tray. Boffey hadn't had the time to toss them away, when one morning a high-ranking marketing executive came into the lab. The bigwig asked about the drops and Boffey explained that they were castoffs from his work.

Undeterred, the exec asked him to add some additional flavors and colors to the rejects and bring them to his office. The scientist complied and the result was one of the United Kingdom's most popular treats. Boffey never received a medal of honor for his meritorious candy service—but such a lack of adulation never bothered him. Boffey gave it so little thought that years later he couldn't even pinpoint the day of his momentous discovery.

"I didn't even write it in my diary," he told a local newspaper decades after Jelly Tots were introduced to the world in 1967. "I was about twenty-eight at the time and so busy with all the other products I was working on that I didn't pay much attention to it."

Over the years he's told people about his claim to fame, receiving one of two very different reactions. He joked, "They either hug me for keeping their children happy for however many minutes or give me a slap for ruining their teeth."

PEZ: Antismoking mint

PEZ was definitely not intended for children when it was invented. With sexy ladies featured prominently in advertising and a message aimed at smokers, we can only hope kids were the furthest thing from Austrian inventor Eduard Haas's mind when he came up with the product in 1927.

The scion of a successful entrepreneurial family, Haas was following in the footsteps of his grandfather, who had invented a baking powder that made cakes lighter, and his dad, who was a successful wholesale grocer. For his part, Haas developed a cold-pressed sugar brick—much like the shape and size of PEZ today. He added a drop of peppermint oil and figured he had a sophisticated mint that would appeal to the European elite.

Selling them in tins, Haas marketed PEZ (named after the first, middle, and last letters of the German word for peppermint—*pfefferminz*) as "a luxury confection for wealthy people." Haas, who was described as a health enthusiast at the time, thought these mints could also serve as an alternative to lighting up. He sent pretty pill-box-hat-wearing Pez Girls around Europe touting the slogan "Smoking prohibited, PEZing allowed." Following World War II, Haas ratcheted up his commitment to PEZ as an antismoking tool for soldiers who had increasingly used nicotine during the war. Haas hired an engineer named  Oskar Uxa in 1948 to develop a gadget technically dubbed a "pocket article dispensing container." These contraptions looked a lot like a thin lighter—a la the Bic variety—but instead of providing a flame, the spring-loaded machine doled out PEZ. For some reason, Haas believed that eating mints from a fake—albeit chic—lighter would deter smokers all the more.

The little mints inside Uxa's creation remained far from the sweet confection we know today. Some of the early flavors included the very unappealing chlorophyll, eucalyptus, and coffee (how coffee qualifies as a mint is beyond me). In 1953 Haas brought his business to the United States and tried to replicate his marketing approach. Beyond the antismoking shtick, PEZ was now being sold as a way to reclaim self-esteem lost with bad breath and as a tool for staving off hunger, which would help users lose weight. Somehow it was also going to help fight infections (presumably because the dispenser avoided the need for one person to hand over the mint to another, enhancing hygiene).

While these PEZ bricks may have satisfied European customers, Americans had a completely different take. This probably wasn't because of the wild claims of the mint's restorative powers, but due to a far more capitalistic factor: It just cost too much. At the time, a candy bar went for five cents compared to a PEZ dispenser with two refills, which cost a heady twenty-five cents.

Haas turned to his man in America, Curtis Allina, to come up with a solution. Allina, an Austrian who had been raised in the United States, suggested reformulating the brand into a kids' sweet. Thanks to Uxa's antismoking dispenser, Haas' company was positioned to differentiate itself from competitors. They used Uxa's basic design to create a toy that could also give out candy (what could be better?). At first, PEZ came in true toy shapes like a full-body Santa Claus, a full-body robot, or a space gun. But in the late 1950s, the company returned to its sleeker design and began sticking heads on the old faux lighters. Popeye was the first to get the honor in 1958.

Though PEZ has weathered some ups and downs since, popular culture—through movies like *Stand By Me* and TV shows such as *Seinfeld*—have kept it in the public consciousness. Another key to its staying power has been nostalgia fiends. Beginning in the late 1980s, the dispensers were deemed collector worthy. Today more than three billion pieces of PEZ are consumed annually in the United States. Still, it's unlikely that any of those little bricks has prevented smoking.

Pop Rocks: Failed drink additive

If there were an urban legend hall of fame, Pop Rocks would be a slam dunk inductee. No, Mikey from those old Life cereal commercials did not meet a terrible end after eating the carbonated candy, and spider eggs were never found in packets of the sugary pebbles. It's also perfectly safe to wolf down some Pop Rocks and swig a Coke. As absurd as those claims might sound today, there is one seeming tall tale that's actually true: Pop Rocks were invented when an effort to create a convenient way to carbonate Kool-Aid failed.

The man responsible for putting a fizzy chemical reaction in your mouth was Bill Mitchell. He was one of General Foods' most impressive scientists having helped develop such winning products as Cool Whip, Jell-O Instant Pudding, and Angel Food Cake mix. "Throughout the industry," wrote Marv Rudolph in his book *Pop Rocks: The Inside Story of America's Revolutionary Candy*, "Bill [had] a reputation as a true inventor—the sort of person who looks at problems differently and can find elegant, sometimes simple solutions that no one else considered."

Despite that esteem, there was one project that vexed the masterful Mitchell. In 1953, General Foods purchased Kool-Aid. It was a successful brand but didn't do the business of heavyweights Pepsi and Coca-Cola. Mitchell's mission was to come up with a way to mix Kool-Aid and then add a tablet or some other agent to make it bubble like its big boy soft drink competitors.

Mitchell figured carbon dioxide trapped in frozen water could do the trick. He developed a little briquette of chocolate-covered carbonated ice that was dubbed Soda Burst. The idea was you could buy it in the freezer section and then add either water or milk, which would melt the little frozen puck and yield a chocolate soda. The problem was most supermarket freezer sections kept their coolers at unreliable temperatures. When it got too warm, the ice would "de-gas" and the briquettes wouldn't do their job. A second effort required a special contraption that was deemed way too complicated.

After those failures, the scientist shifted gears. Instead of frozen water, he looked for something that could store carbon dioxide at room temperature. He went with sorbitol, a sugar alcohol that occurs naturally in fruit. Unfortunately, the result of his work wasn't a thick solid but a glassy substance that had some fizzle—but not nearly enough to get Kool-Aid popping.

What could have been disappointment turned a light on in Mitchell's mind. If he added a few ingredients to his thin sheet of sorbitol, like everybody's favorite artificial colors and flavors, he could make a new type of carbonated candy. In 1957 he produced the first Pop Rocks.

So did General Foods bigwigs laud Mitchell for his new confection? Let's leave it to one of Mitchell's contemporaries to answer that question. "Carbonated candy was almost a joke; a novelty; a technical curiosity, not a technical accomplishment," said longtime General Foods executive Adolphus Clausi in an interview years later. "Marketing, when shown the product, laughed and said, 'Don't you have something better to do?'"

Yikes. With that frosty reception, no wonder no one considered it a commercial option for nearly two decades. For years, the only people who got a taste were General Foods employees and their kids, who would often ask Mitchell to prepare a batch for birthday parties.

What saved Pop Rocks was a guy named Herman Neff, who sold his Canadian snack company to General Foods in the early 1970s. Neff, who continued to work with General Foods after the sale, found out about Mitchell's popping candy and thought it would sell well north of the US border. He was right. Following that success, it hit the American market in 1976 and became an immediate best seller.

Why the fizzy sweet became such a magnet for fictional stories is unclear. Heck, it didn't even have the Internet to spread false rumors. But the danger claims did frustrate Mitchell, who in 1979 took the unusual step of writing open letters to parents and schools about the safety of Pop Rocks (which were also known as Cosmic Candy). Mitchell even addressed the Mikey rumor, telling customers that "we checked on 'Mikey's' well-being and found he is alive and well."

Popsicles: Cold night and forgetful kid

All Frank Epperson wanted was a cool drink. On a red-letter date (now lost in the mists of time) in 1905, he was sitting on his back porch using a stick to mix together some dry flavored powder into a glass of soda water. For one reason or another, he became distracted. This shouldn't be surprising because Epperson was just eleven years old at the time. Maybe his mother called him; maybe he went to play some ball; or, maybe he simply lost interest in the drink, which by some accounts had lost its fizz.

Whatever the case may be, when he was called into the house that evening he left the mixture outside. It would have been a forgotten mistake if not for the fact that it was an unexpectedly ultrafrigid evening that night in Northern California's Bay Area where Epperson grew up. The next day he came out to find his drink frozen with the stirring stick poking out.

Epperson tasted the combination and loved it. But what was an eleven-year-old to do? He apparently showed his friends (I'm sure it made him very popular at recess), but basically put the idea in the freezer—so to speak.

He would go on to serve as a pilot in World War I and embark on a number of business ventures from real estate to manufacturing kewpie dolls. But in the early 1920s, he noticed that ice-cream sandwiches were becoming a popular treat.

While frozen fruit juice treats, called "hokeypokeys," had been around since the 1870s with vendors successfully selling them on the streets of New York and other big cities, Epperson figured his creative advantage would be that stirring stick he'd left in his soda mixture as a preteen. He filed for a patent for "a handled, frozen confection" in 1923 and began selling his treat, which he first called "the Epsicle"—a combo of his last name and icicle—at a popular local amusement area called Idora Park in Oakland. (Useless fun fact: The wood of choice for the ice treat's stick was and remains birch.) It was a hit and he sold the rights to make his ice lollies to a New York manufacturer called the Joe Lowe Company.

One of the first orders of business around the time Epperson partnered with Joe Lowe was to alter the product's name for marketing purposes. The most popular story surrounding the choice of "Popsicle" asserted that Epperson's children called it "pop's icicle" rather than its real name. This was no small marketing sample as he had nine kids, so this tale could very well be true. Others suggest that the name was simply a variation on another sweet that used a stick: the lollipop.

Regardless, the product quickly became a nationwide favorite and by 1928, sixty million of the treats were sold. With royalties rolling in, Epperson's childhood discovery looked to be an annuity for life. Sadly, the Depression changed that course. Being an entrepreneur at heart and always in need of money for his next venture, he ended up selling his stake in his invention in 1929.

Little did he know that during the Depression, a double-Popsicle with two sticks, which allowed friends to break apart the ice treat and share the cooling confection for very little cost, would become an even bigger hit and cemented the Popsicle's place in most Americans' memories of childhood. (In one 2005 survey adults said that the Popsicle—rather than the ice-cream cone or the ice-cream sandwich—was the treat they most often purchased as a child.)

Later in life Epperson, who died in 1983 at age eighty-nine, would have mixed emotions about his accidental discovery. On the one hand, he clearly regretted his decision to sell out. "I was flat and had to liquidate all my assets," he once said. "I haven't been the same since." But he did always appreciate his place in snack lore—which undoubtedly made him a hit with his more than two dozen grandchildren. "It has given a lot of simple pleasure to a lot of people," he said in 1973 on the fiftieth anniversary of the Popsicle. "And I've enjoyed being part of it all."

Potato Chips: Take-no-guff chef

Sussing out the origins of the potato chip can be as messy as digging your hand into a bag of the ubiquitous snack food.

For decades one particular story has been the darling of most authors, journalists, and potato chip industry professionals. It revolves around a larger-than-life chef from Saratoga Springs, New York, named George Crum. The son of an African-American father and a Native American mother, Crum was renowned as a top-notch cook in the fancy resort town in upstate New York. During his career, he would serve such luminaries as presidents Chester A. Arthur and Grover Cleveland.

In 1853 Crum was working as the head chef at one of the area's most exclusive hotels, Moon's Lake House. On one summer evening, a prominent guest—some claimed it was the uber-wealthy Cornelius Vanderbilt—ordered french-fried potatoes. Back then these thick-cut slices of the starchy tuber were a dish of the rich. Thomas Jefferson discovered them while serving as ambassador to France in the 1700s and brought them back to the United States, offering the potatoes to company at Monticello. On the night in question, the guest (whether it be Vanderbilt or another well-heeled patron) thought the potatoes were either too soggy or not flavorful enough for consumption and sent them back to the kitchen.

Even when it came to the well-heeled and famous, Crum was not a man to be trifled with. It was said that he once forced industry barons William Vanderbilt and Jay Gould to wait more than an hour while other guests who had arrived earlier got seated first. Crum was clear about his skills: He could cook a dinner "fit for a king," but if there was a complaint he could also present "the most indigestible substitutes [he] could contrive."

In this case, the complaint from the dining room meant that he was going to provide what he thought would be the latter. He sliced the potatoes so thin that when fried they would come out too crispy to pick up with a fork. He then added so much salt that there could be no complaint about it being bland. The tale concludes with the guest trying Crum's attempt at indigestible and loving it. From then on, the dish— named Saratoga Chips—was included on the menu as a house special.

As great as this story is, there is some evidence it's more legend than reality. While most everyone agrees that the chip did find its start in Saratoga Springs, Crum may have only been a bit player in its invention—and the tale of battling a rich eater apocryphal. Author Dirk Burhans offers a compelling case on this front in his book *Crunch! A History of the Great American Potato Chip*. Burhans points out that while Crum was not a man short on confidence, he never claimed he came up with potato chips. In fact, that contention didn't really enter print until the 1940s. As for the upset customer anecdote, it didn't become popular until the 1970s.

Still, even if Crum's lucky run-in with a snotty guest isn't true, it's quite possible that the potato chip was an accidental find. Burhans suggests that the "most credible" origins explanation did come from the kitchen of Moon's Lake House. But it was Crum's sister, Katie Speck Wicks, who made the discovery. "Aunt Katie," wrote Burhans, "was frying crullers and peeling potatoes at the same time. A thin slice of potato found its way into the frying oil for the crullers, and Katie fished it out." Crum saw the chip, took a taste, and was pleased. After Katie explained how it happened, Crum supposedly said, "That's a good accident. We'll have plenty of these." While Crum's local obituary in 1914 didn't mention the chip, Katie's obit three years later credited her with its creation.

Other explanations exist as well. Still, the popular disgruntled patron story has never been definitively disproved, leaving some hope that Crum's tale of trying to stick it to the rich man may have truly happened.

Pretzels: Holy rewards

If author Dan Brown ever needs new grist for a *Da Vinci Code*–type book, he might consider munching on some pretzels. The snack has Catholic roots shrouded in the fog of food lore.

One popular story about the pretzel's religious invention stars a monk in either Northern Italy or Southern France (already we're getting a bit hazy). It was circa AD 610 and the religious man's job was making bread. One day, he had excess dough after completing his work and wasn't sure what to do with it. Giving it just a moment's thought, he decided to roll the dough into a new shape to make gifts for small children who had successfully learned their prayers. The pretzel's distinctive design was meant to represent two folded arms. Back then folding arms, rather than clasping or putting hands together,

was the common posture for praying. The monk allegedly dubbed his creation the *pretiola*, which is Latin for "little reward."

An alternative to the story ditches the monk and has the dawn of pretzels occurring approximately two centuries earlier. In this one, Roman Christians, who abstained from meat and dairy products during the forty days of Lent, needed a nonoffending food option. The pretzel was made to serve that role and, again, the shape was to remind religious adherents to focus on prayer. The original name in this account was *bracellae* (Latin for "little arms"). According to the Catholic Education Resource Center, there is a fifth century illustration of a pretzel-like product in the Vatican Library but no recipe to corroborate this early birth (for those of you who want to get on this mystery, check out Codex 3867).

While those are the most popular tales, others exist. There's one that says monks made the strangely shaped bread to allow for pilgrims to easily hang it on their walking staffs. An alternative claims a German king decreed loaves of bread be made in a way to allow the sun to shine through them three different ways. Why he wanted this is unclear. Whichever you believe, the pretzel was a popular purchase at the local marketplace in Germany by the Middle Ages. At that point it was known by an Old High German word, *bretzitella*, and then *brezel* (or *bretzel*, depending on who you believe) before transforming into its modern name.

The Christian storytelling surrounding the pretzel doesn't end there. It's said that pretzels saved Vienna from Muslim invaders in 1529. The Ottoman Turks were laying siege to the European capital and devised a plan to dig tunnels underneath the sturdy city walls in the middle of the night. What the Turks didn't know was bakers labored through the night cooking pretzels in order to have fresh bread ready for morning customers. These men supposedly heard the below-ground commotion and alerted authorities. As a result, the Turks were repelled, preventing Muslim rule in Europe.

This romantic recounting is very unlikely. It's true that the Ottomans tried to tunnel under the walls in order to lay mines to destroy the city's protection, but, according to the book *Besieged: An Encyclopedia of Great Sieges from Ancient Times to the Present*, it was an Ottoman deserter who warned the Austrians about the digging plans.

So what ties between the pretzel and the Christian faith are worthy of our devotion? Some in Europe, along with members of the Pennsylvania Dutch in the United States, have put pretzels on Christmas trees as decorations and hidden them as prizes at Easter (a la Easter eggs). They have also been used at wedding ceremonies, where the baked good is broken apart in a wishbone-like game. As for the rest of it, I leave it to Dan Brown to figure out how to weave it all together in *The Pretzel Code*.

Twinkies: Strawberry afterthought

Devoted fans of the ubiquitous Twinkie should give praise to the ever-so-wholesome strawberry for the confection's invention. It was the strawberry's relatively short season for freshness that inspired the spongy American icon.

In 1930 James Dewar was working as a Hostess bakery manager in Schiller Park, Illinois, a Chicago suburb. Times were tight and the company wanted to come up with a low-priced product that would appeal to Depression-starved consumers. Cue the strawberry. Dewar's factory used them as part of a little finger cake product they were selling. But the problem was strawberries would only stay sweet for six weeks so the cakes came and went quickly. As a result, the bakery molds used for the strawberry treats sat idle for most of the year.

Looking to maximize those pans, Dewar, a longtime bakery man who entered the business in 1920 as a wagon driver, concocted the Twinkie. He named it after a billboard he saw for a company called

Twinkle Toe Shoes on a trip to St. Louis. ("I shortened it to make it a little zippier for the kids," he said.) The new cakes, which went on the market at a nickel for two, weren't like the yellow wonders we taste today. Dewar originally kept with the fruit theme, creating a creamy banana filling. The key: unlike strawberries, fresh bananas could be found throughout the year.

The Twinkie was an immediate success, but it needed another unexpected turn to reach its full height of popularity. During World War II rationing made it impossible to source enough bananas to keep the production lines going. With little choice, Hostess was forced to come up with an alternative—the creamy vanilla-flavored insides used today. After the war, there was no need to return to the banana flavor as the new center proved more popular than its predecessor. Nowadays some 500 million Twinkies are sold annually. As for the banana cream, it has been used in limited runs with much success.

Sure enough, over the years, the Twinkie has become a foundational item in American pop culture. Archie Bunker described it as "WASP Soul Food" on the hit 1970s TV show *All in the Family,* and there are even Twinkie recipes for such varied dishes as Twinkie Pancakes and Twinkie Sushi. Not surprisingly considering his then-penchant for sweets, President Bill Clinton included a package in a 1999 time capsule celebrating the millennium. While some may think disposable Twinkies are an odd addition for a time capsule, think again. A Maine teacher once claimed he kept a perfectly good-looking Twinkie next to the chalkboard in his classroom for thirty years (Hostess sort of ruins that party, asserting their cake really only has a shelf-life of about twenty-five days). The treat's darkest hour—beyond when nutritionists take potshots at it—came when Dan White, who murdered San Francisco mayor George Moscone and supervisor Harvey Milk in 1978, said his intake of junk food was evidence of the depression that led to the killings. The media dubbed it the "Twinkie Defense."

Yet, through it all, Dewar stood by his strawberry-inspired (or lack thereof) creation. "Some people say Twinkies are the quintessential junk food, but I believe in the things," he said decades after the invention. "I fed them to my four kids, and they feed them to my fifteen grandchildren. My boy Jimmy played football for the Cleveland Browns. My other son, Bobby, played quarterback for the University of Rochester. Twinkies never hurt them." As Dewar lived to the ripe old age of eighty-eight on a diet that regularly included the spongy treat he may very well have been right.

Additives and Extras

Alka-Seltzer: Newspaper discovery

The biggest story a journalist at the *Elkhart Truth* ever broke never made it into print. In December 1928, the small northern Indiana town of Elkhart was hit by a countrywide cold and influenza epidemic. Businesses in the area were barely staying open with so many employees calling in sick.

One day during the outbreak, Andrew H. "Hub" Beardsley made a trip over to the *Truth*, a local community newspaper, to have a friendly chat with its managing editor Tom Keene. Hub and his brother Charles ran Dr. Miles Medical Company, a local business specializing in remedies. Their big seller was something called Dr. Miles' Nervine, which allegedly treated such "nervous" ailments as headaches, backaches, epilepsy, and sleeplessness. They also sold Dr. Miles' Cactus Compound for heart ailments (it might have helped the heart, but with its main ingredient being 23 proof alcohol, it's unclear what it did to the rest of the body). Despite some success the Beardsley brothers were really looking for a bubbling concoction, known as an "effervescence," that could be a cure-all.

While Hub wasn't searching for his answer when he walked into the *Truth* that day, he did notice something peculiar. None of the newspaper's employees were absent. Shockingly, they all seemed to be working away as if the flu scourge had passed them by. Hub was intrigued and asked Keene how this was possible. Keene delivered the monumental scoop: He pulled out a mixture of aspirin, bicarbonate, and lemon juice and explained that whenever an employee began feeling sick, he'd just mix up the bubbly combination. Instantly Hub knew he'd found the product he'd been searching for.

He went back to his laboratory and charged his chief chemist, Maurice Trencer, with putting the elements of the *Truth*'s magic elixir into a tablet. Within a week, the scientist had created Aspir-Vess, which was later renamed Alka-Seltzer. (The new name combined "alkaline," a term for an acid-repelling element, with the popular fizzy drink "seltzer.") While the product was marketed for a number of ailments, including such far-flung problems as exhaustion and a bad temper, from a food-and-drink perspective it became a go-to item for upset stomachs and hangovers.

But more than even its medicinal qualities, Alka-Seltzer became a triumph in marketing. Hub's brother Charles invested heavily in sponsoring radio shows, which gave the product a huge bounce. Later, their television commercials proved to be classics. There was Speedy, the tablet's cartoon spokesperson, who whisked around with a wand making people feel better. An ad depicting a man offering the post-meal lament "I can't believe I ate that whole thing" was a huge winner in the 1970s and the mantra "plop, plop, fizz, fizz/ oh what a relief it is" became ubiquitous in the 1980s. The catchphrase "That's a spicy meatball" was also part of an Alka-Seltzer campaign.

In large part, the success of Alka-Seltzer made Elkhart a very prosperous locale. At one point, the town reportedly featured forty millionaires—or approximately one in every thousand residents. Alas, Alka-Seltzer and its parent company, which were purchased by Bayer AG in 1977, have since moved the main office. In 2009 Elkhart earned the dubious distinction of having the fastest increasing jobless rate in the United States, jumping from 4.7 percent to 15.3 percent in a single year. Sadly, there are some ills that even a couple of Alka-Seltzer tablets cannot cure.

Artificial Sweeteners: Sloppy scientists

You'd think that rule number one when working with chemical compounds in a lab would be don't taste anything unless you're absolutely certain what you're putting in your mouth. After all, we even tell little kids on the playground to follow that rule. But for those who can't get through the day without a Diet Pepsi or a Coke Zero, it's fortunate that apparently many scientists aren't too worried about following that childhood missive.

Each of the original holy trinity of artificial sweeteners—saccharin, cyclamate, and aspartame (aka NutraSweet)—was discovered by researchers who just didn't think to wash their hands. As for the most recent, and today's most popular, artificial sweetener, sucralose (known on the street as Splenda), it has its own different but equally accidental origin story.

Saccharin was the original sugar substitute. In 1879 one of the century's most revered chemists, Ira Remsen, was doing research on coal tar derivatives. (If you wonder why saccharin has that awful aftertaste, coal derivatives might give you some sense.) During research, an associate, Constantin Fahlberg, accidentally spilled some of a substance he was preparing on his hands. Overcome by intellectual curiosity—rather than common sense—he took a lick and found it to be incredibly flavorful. It turned out that the mixture was 300 times as sweet as basic sugar. He named it saccharin after the Latin word for sugarcane, *saccharum*.

While saccharin went on the market as an alternative to sugar, its bitter aftertaste did somewhat limit its value. What was needed was another sweetener to mix with it that could lessen the bite. Cyclamate, which was discovered in 1937, wasn't as sweet as saccharin, but proved to be its potential partner (though some studies have indicated the combo can cause cancer). Yet again, its discovery came from another messy scientist.

Michael Sveda was a student at the University of Illinois working on some sulfamates that were expected to have promising pharmacological properties. He got his hands dirty—so to speak—mixing these compounds and didn't think anything of it when he went for a cigarette break. After taking a long drag from his smoke, he noticed something very odd: Chemicals on his hands from the experiments had soaked into the cigarette creating a sweet taste.

Proving that scientists don't always learn from the past, James M. Schlatter had his own unclean story when it came to finding the combination that led to Equal and NutraSweet. In December 1965, after getting some aspartame powder on his hands, he licked a finger in order to help pick up a piece of paper. He noticed the strong sweet taste (some 200 times greater than sugar).

Shashikant Phadnis's mistake, which led to Splenda, wasn't a product of poor cleanliness. It was due to miscommunication. In 1975, the native of India was a student at Queen Elizabeth College in London working on an experiment with a highly toxic chemical called sulfuryl chloride. At one point in the proceedings, Phadnis's adviser asked him to "test" his work. Maybe it was the professor's British accent, but the student thought he said to "taste" his work. Despite the toxicity, the dutiful student followed orders. Panicked, the teacher asked if Phadnis was crazy. But fears soon turned to excitement when it turned out that the mixture's toxicity had been neutralized and the result was a calorie-free powder 200 times sweeter than sugar.

Baking Powder: Adoring husband

Baking powder doesn't seem like a building block for romance. But the invention of this product—which would become a fantastic yeast substitute for making bread, biscuits, and muffins—was essentially a love letter to a woman. The yearning man who channeled his feelings was Alfred Bird. A pharmacist from England's Birmingham area, Bird set up his own shop in 1837 dispensing the usual elixirs and medicines.

The new business kept the twenty-four-year-old Bird busy, but the man had something more important to consider. He'd recently married and, unfortunately, his fair wife Elizabeth wasn't the stoutest of individuals. Most notably, she suffered from digestive problems, making bread products nearly impossible to enjoy. That wouldn't do for the newlywed Bird. He resolved to devise some way for his bride to enjoy scones and morning toast.

It didn't happen overnight, but in 1843 Bird came up with a substance he called "Fermenting Powder." Later renamed baking powder, the stuff did the trick. Not only could Elizabeth enjoy bread without tummy troubles, but the results were also lighter and fluffier than many traditional breads. Bird then matched his marital devotion with an impressive business sense. He invested heavily on marketing, giving away free calendars featuring ads for his powder. One of his favorite mottos was "Early to Bed, Early to Rise, Stick to Your Work and Advertise."

Beyond the paying public, he was also able to convince Her Majesty's armed forces that his invention would be perfect for baking fresh bread on military fronts and for hospital patients, whose diets might be limited by injury during the Crimean War. Bird would seal the deal with the Duke of Newcastle, who was the country's prime minister at the time, by personally making five loaves to prove his product's integrity.

His wife's infirmity paid dividends with baking powder, but it wasn't the only time Elizabeth's maladies made Bird rich. Along with her inability to eat regular bread (problem solved), Mrs. Bird was also allergic to eggs. One dish she particularly longed for was custard. The loving Bird went to work again. He created a custard using corn flour instead of eggs as the basis. Easy to prepare and as tasty as the real thing, the new custard was wildly successful, especially in times of war when eggs were scarce.

Bird never stopped tinkering. He came up with an oil-powered lamp that could be refilled while still on and he liked to study storm patterns with the use of a huge barometer he hung in one of his stores. Neither of those were money makers like his powders, demonstrating nothing inspires like love for a good—albeit sickly—woman.

Corn Starch: Indomitable chemist

Admittedly, corn starch isn't the sexiest entry in this book. For those readers who spend more time eating than cooking, it's a valuable ingredient for thickening gravies, sauces, and puddings. While its purpose may yield a yawn, the story of its discovery is a compelling combination of perseverance and a dash of luck at just the right time.

Starches date back at least two thousand years. Their production is a painstaking process that requires a complicated combination of steps to extract the substance. In the early days, wheat and potatoes were primarily used in starch production. Yet, even then, only small amounts could be removed. It was such a costly endeavor that during the reign of Queen Elizabeth I, there was a law that prevented the use of starch for any purpose other than to style wigs and stiffen the ruffles worn by the queen and her court. Over time innovations in the manufacturing process increased production enough for other everyday uses.

In the 1830s Thomas Kingsford was aware of the labor-intensive process required to make starches. A British native, Kingsford had immigrated to the United States to seek his fortune. While in England he'd worked as both a baker and at a chemical factory, and when he arrived in America, he took a job at a starch plant in New Jersey. Kingsford was convinced that the wheat the company was using would never yield enough starch to make big money. He beseeched his bosses to try maize (aka Indian corn). His colleagues laughed at him.

Kingsford was undeterred. He began doing his own research at home. He borrowed equipment from locals and for years tried everything he could think of to extract starch from corn. One day, long into his efforts, he experimented by mixing corn mush with wood-ash lye. It didn't work and Kingsford dumped the work in the garbage. He next tried to combine the corn with a solution of lime. Again, he experienced failure. Surely discouraged by this point, he dumped this combination in the same tub and took a break from the whole process.

Sometime later, Kingsford was ready to go at it again. But before setting off in a new direction, he decided to clean up. He picked up the tub from his previous efforts and began emptying it when he noticed something. At the bottom of the garbage was pure, perfectly separated white starch. The unintended combination of the discarded lye and lime with the corn had yielded exactly what he'd been searching for all these years.

In 1842 he went to market with his new starch, which was easier to produce in large quantities than any previous option. At times in Kingsford's life, he'd taken jobs to support his widowed mother and even initially moved to the United States without his family to make sure he could earn enough money to take care of them. Within less time than it took him to make his discovery, Kingsford was a rich man. In 1848 his new company produced 1.3 million pounds of starch, and by 1859 the annual output was 7 million pounds.

Hot Dog Bun: Small carts and glove thieves

The hot dog is without a doubt the greatest contribution German immigrants have ever made to the American food scene. (Sorry, boosters of stollen or fans of German red cabbage; it's true.) As one would expect, the frankfurter, a slender smoked cousin of the bratwurst, originated in the German town of Frankfurt centuries before German-Americans began selling them in the United States in the 1800s.

While those sausages were very popular on their own, what turned them into American icons—think baseball, apple pie, and Chevrolet—was the bun, which made the meal an on-the-go favorite from ballparks to boardwalks. (Fun fact: Yale students were among the first to use the term "hot dog" in 1895. Presumably it was because the tube meat reminded them of another German import—the dachshund.)

So where did the hot dog bun come from? Many give that honor to a Coney Island man named Charles Feltman in 1871. According to writer Jeffrey Stanton, Feltman's customers wanted hot sandwiches, but the New York butcher's pie cart was too small to pack a variety of options on his rounds. In need of a simple alternative he came up with the idea of turning his slim sausages into sandwiches by using an elongated roll. New York was a hub for hot dogs and along with Feltman, a baker by the name of Ignatz Frischmann, who was a Feltman contemporary, has also been floated as the bun inventor by at least one scholar.

That said the New Yorkers aren't the only people to stake a claim to the indispensible bun's marriage to the hot dog. The other main contender provides a far more colorful explanation for the bready addition.

Anton Ludwig Feuchtwanger was a German-American vendor in St. Louis, who sold sausages in the days before the hot dog moniker. He called them "red hots," and in 1883 he recognized the difficulty of eating the tube meat by hand. His solution: providing his customers with white gloves to wear while enjoying his goods. The gloves would keep patrons' hands clean, help avoid scalding from the sizzling sausage, and add a little class to the affair. Solving one problem led to another: a frustrated Feuchtwanger discovered some less scrupulous buyers were walking off with the gloves. He grew weary of the cost of replacing them. So the vendor went to a local baker (some say it was his brother-in-law) and the result was an inexpensive soft bun.

No doubt, Feuchtwanger's story feels a bit too flavorful. After all, reusing gloves doesn't sound too hygienic. If he was doing good business, his laundry bills must have been crushing. Nevertheless, many publications have given Feuchtwanger recognition for the invention. *The Oxford Companion to Food* lists both Feuchtwanger and Feltman as inventors and doesn't pass judgment on which vendor deserves acclaim. (The book, unlike most who discuss Feuchtwanger, avoids the glove tale.)

Even if he wasn't the first and his glove story was more marketing myth than reality, Feuchtwanger positively played a role in making the bun a staple in the Midwest. At the 1904 World's Fair in his hometown of St. Louis, Feuchtwanger was a popular concessionaire who did really well with his hot dog-plus-bun combination. Feuchtwanger's stand was so popular that years later many erroneously attribute his glove story to that event. Thus, even if Feltman came first, Feuchtwanger and his efforts definitely helped expand the love for sausage on a bun.

Ice-Cream Cone: Debatable world's fair find

The ice-cream cone's origin is considered by many to be as muddied as a thick scoop of Rocky Road. Nevertheless, according to the

International Ice Cream Association, there is an official tale, which goes like this:

It all took place at the 1904 St. Louis World's Fair (aka the Louisiana Purchase Exposition). There had previously been similar events of epic scale, but nothing compared to this Missouri attraction, which inspired the Judy Garland film classic *Meet Me in St. Louis*. Not only did it host the Olympic Games and attract some twenty million people over a seven-month span, but it was also credited with popularizing, among other edible delights, the ice-cream cone.

Enter Syrian-born Ernest Hamwi. A recent immigrant to the United States, he set up a concession stand at the fair hoping to entice patrons with *zalabia*, a crisp round waffle-like pastry from his home country. Next to Hamwi's spot was an ice-cream vendor—one of the fifty or so at the exposition. The seminal moment came on a particularly hot day when Hamwi's neighbor ran out of bowls and faced a line of customers with no way to provide ice cream. Hamwi stepped in, reshaping his zalabia into a cone. The creation provided customers with a way to enjoy the treat and the day was saved. From then on he named it the "World's Fair Cornucopia." It spread to other concessionaires and the rest is history.

The only problem: Not everyone endorses that history. We can confirm Hamwi did establish a cone business, the Missouri Cone Company, in 1910. But food experts have been hard-pressed to corroborate any of his 1904 story. Further complicating the matter is a handful of different vendors from the fair who also take credit. A Norfolk, Virginia, restaurant owner named Albert Doumar has long claimed his uncle Abe was the one to modify a zalabia and come up with the conical confection. He even wrote a dramatically named book about it called *The Saga of the Ice Cream Cone*.

Then there are two different sets of brothers—Nick and Albert Kabbaz and Charles and Frank Menches. The Kabbazes were Syrian immigrants, who allegedly worked for Hamwi. They supposedly showed their boss how to turn the zalabia into an ice-cream holder. Charles Menches claims he came up with it to impress a lady (in contrast, some assert that the Menches brothers were the ice-cream vendors next door to Hamwi who benefited from his inspiration). The Menches family was an early adopter as they did start their own cone company just one year after the fair. Another claimant was the Turkish-born David Avayou, who said he was inspired by French paper or metal cones.

If all that wasn't enough, an Italian-American named Italo Marchiony patented his own cone-like ice-cream holder the year *before* the 1904 fair. Still, some argue that Marchiony's creation wasn't really a cone. "He actually patented this mold that made little pastry cups," according to food author Anne Cooper Funderburg. "They looked like tea cups." One final contestant: Agnes Bertha Marshall, a British writer who included an entry for "cornets with cream" in an 1888 cookbook (a cornet remains British-speak for an ice-cream cone).

Are you confused yet? So was Dairy Queen when it wanted to celebrate the one hundredth anniversary of the cone and ended up doing it twice—once in 2003 in honor of Marchiony and a second time in 2004 to recognize the impact the St. Louis World's Fair had on the cone. (Apologies, Agnes—your effort didn't get props from the ice-cream chain.)

As for who at the fair really deserves credit, it's a conundrum so great that, on a slow news day in 2004, the *Chicago Tribune* devoted an editorial to the topic.

"Many of the cone-creation tales involved coming up with something on the spot to hold ice cream," the newspaper wrote. "So while the paternity of the cone may be unclear, necessity was clearly the mother of this invention. It just may be that more than one fair vendor or patron needed emergency ice cream assistance at the same time in St. Louis 100 years ago."

In the end, it's clear the *Chicago Tribune*, like many, didn't want to get their hands sticky with this one.

Maple Syrup: Native American domestic clash

Check out any website devoted to maple syrup making and you're bound to come across the origin story of the Iroquois chief Woksis and his wife Moqua. The legend usually goes as follows: Woksis had thrown his tomahawk into a maple tree one night just before going to bed. The next morning he pulled it out and left to go on a hunt. It was unseasonably warm on this March day and from the tomahawk gash warm maple syrup began trickling down the tree into a pot that happened to be luckily located on the ground below. When it came time for Moqua to fetch water to boil in preparation for dinner, she noticed the liquid in the pot and figured she could save a trip down to the creek. Woksis returned home with some venison, they boiled it up and, eureka, the sweetness of the meal spurred them and other Native Americans to begin cutting into trees to extract the sweet nectar.

Is there any truth to the story? We are certain many Native American tribes produced maple syrup before the arrival of European settlers. The Algonquin called the maple sugar *sinzibukwud* (meaning "drawn from wood") and the Ojibways named it *sheesheegummawis* ("sap flows fast"). In addition, tomahawks might have been used to cut gashes in maple trees as part of the extraction process. Tribes were known to use sharp instruments, rather than spigots utilized by Westerners, to get the sap out.

As for Woksis and Moqua's role, the story appears to have gotten its start in modern literature from an 1896 *Atlantic Monthly* article written by Rowland E. Robinson. His telling of the tale isn't quite as, well, sweet as the current narrative. Robinson depicts Woksis as a grump who before going off to "the chase" for the day tells his wife to cook up some moose meat. He warns her that if she does a bad job "she might be reminded of the time he stuck a stake in the snow." (I'm not sure what that means, but it doesn't sound good.) Moqua promises "strict compliance" and starts melting some snow in a pot for water. She then goes about her business making new moccasins for Woksis. Moqua gets so focused on her work that she doesn't notice that the frayed bark cord used to hang the pot over the fire is about to break until it's too late. All the water spills out of the container and Moqua gets nervous and runs outside. There she pulls some sap from a great maple as a water alternative (in this version, the tribe knew about maple juices as a "pleasant drink" but hadn't figured out its broader uses).

Moqua refills the pot, but becomes aghast when she sees the sap has boiled away and the meat has become dark and shriveled. Now she's really freaked out remembering that whole stake-snow thing. She bolts from the dwelling just as the huffy Woksis returns. When she doesn't hear any angry comments from her husband, she returns to find her man in pure syrup heaven. He even goes so far as to break the pot to get the remnants of the treacle.

Could Robinson have gotten it right? His writing in the *Atlantic Monthly* possessed a breathless style that tastes a bit like pure hokum. Still, there are few other competing origin stories and there was at least one contemporary official source that vouched for Robinson's trustworthiness: the Vermont Department of Agriculture. They wrote in 1914 that Robinson told tales of "picture pioneer life in the Green Mountain State with a charm and accuracy equaled by few, and surpassed by none."

Marmalade: Stormy oranges

Marmalade has long been a British breakfast staple. Chunks of Seville oranges mixed with sugar to produce what's known as "chip marmalade" is *the* traditional spread with toast on cold misty mornings from Edinburgh to London. But the first mass producer of the condiment may have never gotten into the business if not for a fortuitously ill-fated voyage.

Janet Keiller was the wife of a store owner in Dundee, Scotland, in the eighteenth century. One day, her husband came home with an odd purchase: Seville oranges. Unlike the sweet succulent fruits our kids eat during halftime at soccer games, these oranges were tart and would have been a tough sell as a peel-and-eat treat. In fact, they were often used at the time as a souring agent for British sauces. Janet was probably confused at the purchase. Her husband likely explained he was being enterprising. The oranges weren't bound for Dundee (historians believe they were on their way to Leith for the markets either there or in Edinburgh). But the ship carrying the cargo had been battered by a storm and was forced to take refuge in Dundee's harbor. Unable to complete its journey, the ship's captain looked to unload some goods at a cut rate.

Now it was up to Janet to make something of this bargain. Marmalade had long been used as a word for a product very different from the spreadable bittersweet confection we know today. The term comes from the Portuguese word *marmelada*, which means quince paste. During the fifteenth and early sixteenth centuries, it was a hard paste that could be cut and served as a dessert. By the end of the sixteenth century all types of fruits, including plums, dates, and strawberries, were being used for this purpose.

Nevertheless, it's likely that Janet was aware of a new kind of smooth spreadable marmalade that had become popular in Scotland in the years around the time of her husband's purchase. But she put her own spin on it. Opting to save on the labor normally required to grind down the oranges, she shred the fruits for a more chunky option. "Janet Keiller did not invent orange marmalade," wrote C. Anne Wilson in *The Book of Marmalade* (yes, there is a definitive tome on this topic). "But she contributed to the establishment of the 'chip' style as Scotland's very own marmalade."

Before long, Janet's jars were flying off the shelves of the family store. Seeing a business opportunity, the Keillers were the first to establish a factory to mass-produce marmalade (some suggest it was Janet's son or even later generations of the family who keyed the business's boom). The working classes liked it because, as a spread on toast, it was an inexpensive form of nourishment. Also, unlike many jams, which were seasonal, the resiliency of the Seville orange meant that marmalade could be produced year-round. From there the delicacy quickly spread and became a must on breakfast tables across the British Empire. By 2010, though, marmalade had transformed into a bit of a relic of a bygone era. One survey found that approximately 80 percent of the spread is sold to people over the age of forty-five. Youthful buyers will have to be found if marmalade hopes to weather the storm once again.

Mayonnaise: Victory spread

To the victor goes the spoils and when it came to eighteenth-century French politician and commander Louis François Armand de Vignerot du Plessis, duc de Richelieu, the spoils were slathered with an improvised new condiment.

With the exception of a couple of World Wars, the French and British have been scrapping on battlefields around the world for centuries. In 1756 the two countries were tussling over the island of

Minorca, off the coast of Spain. The rock had tremendous strategic value so when duc de Richelieu captured its key city, Port Mahon, the French leader was ready to rejoice.

Not that it took too much to get the duke in a celebratory mood. Legend has it that he enjoyed eating dinner in the nude. With this level of commitment to meals plus the added pressure of celebrating a huge win, duc de Richelieu's chef wanted the victory feast to be special.

But according to some food historians, the cook did not have everything he needed to put together the perfect meal.

"[E]vidently, he was lacking some cream to mix with the egg yolks and he used oil instead, and the new sauce became mahonaise, which would be a derivation of Port Mahon," Richard Gutman, curator of the culinary archives and museum at Johnson and Wales University in Providence, Rhode Island, told National Public Radio on the 250th anniversary of the tangy condiment's supposed invention.

The concoction, which was effectively the local Spanish sauce *aioli* minus copious amounts of garlic, was brought back to France where it spread throughout the continent as both a base for other sauces and as a dressing. Keeping with the Anglo-Gallic tensions, the British didn't embrace mayonnaise until around 1841—eighty-five years after it was created—and many Brits insisted on ditching the French moniker and going with the more bland "salad cream" as its name. (Mayonnaise's migration onto sandwiches would be popularized in the United States, where Richard Hellmann was one of the first to begin selling jars of it for that and other purposes in 1912.)

Some food experts have credited other moments in history for mayo's entry into our diets. These have included the town of Bayonne in southwest France (along this line of thinking, bayonnaise was changed to mayonnaise somewhere down the road); ancient French chefs who named it after the old French word *moyeu*, meaning "egg yolk"; and Charles de Lorraine, duc de Mayenne, who supposedly lost a key battle to—you guessed it—the British in the sixteenth century because he took so long finishing a chicken meal doused in the sauce.

There are many more alternate origin tales, which begs the question: Why has duc de Richelieu endured as the most popular explanation? Gutman offers this simple reason: "[T]he Richelieu one is compact and nice and the Mahon makes sense."

Nutella: Post–World War II austerity

Turin is Italy's chocolate capital. "Every chocolatier has his very own chocolate, his own secret recipes, passed down through the generations," one local chocolate maker told a reporter in 2004. "In other cities, chefs get up and make croissants in the morning. In Turin, we get up and make chocolate."

Along with its sweet tooth–inducing industry, the Piedmont region where Turin is located is also known for hazelnuts. *The Oxford Companion to Food* calls the "famous" Tonda Gentile Delle Langhe variety grown in this area Italy's best.

One would assume that these two popular elements—chocolate and hazelnuts—would be a perfect marriage blended for every conceivable use (chocolate-hazelnut pasta anyone?). Think again.

Nutella, the wildly successful hazelnut spread (if you're unfamiliar, just head over to Costco where you can find vats of it), wasn't the result of someone thinking the two would be a natural mix. Its birth was all about necessity.

Hazelnut-infused chocolate is said to date back to the days of Napoleon, but the first commercial combination of the two products came in the mid-1800s when Italians faced quotas on such luxury items as cocoa beans. To overcome the shortage, chocolatiers Paul Caffarel and Michele Prochet replaced some of the pricey cocoa with hazelnuts to create a new type of chocolate. They named their creation

Gianduiotto and it became a standard part of the Turin chocolate scene.

Despite the success of Gianduiotto, the chocolate-hazelnut mix didn't yield any major new products until world events intervened. Following World War II, Italy was in short supply of chocolate. At the same time, the war had limited the country's exports and Piedmont warehouses were overflowing with hazelnuts that hadn't found a home. It was the first matter that concerned Pietro Ferrero, a local chocolate maker. He either didn't have enough or couldn't afford enough chocolate to fill his shelves. So he turned to the second matter—excess hazelnuts—to solve his problem.

In 1946 he combined toasted hazelnuts with cocoa butter, vegetable oil, and cocoa powder to create his own hazelnut confection. This innovation was sold in loaves so pieces could be cut off (like cheese) and put on bread. Ferrero called it *pasta gianduja* (*pasta* for paste and *gianduja* after a famed Piedmontese carnival character). According to one source, he sold an impressive 660 pounds of his creation in one month that year. Initially spurred by limitations on ingredients, Ferrero was now sold on hazelnuts. In 1949 he rolled out a new extra-creamy, spreadable rendering of his invention. He named this version *super-creama gianduja*.

The spread became a must-have at stores where kids would pay to get their bread slathered with the stuff. (In a sort of horror-esque side note, these stores would call their service "The Smearing.") In 1964, as it became popular throughout Europe, the name was changed to Nutella. According to the book *Why Italians Like to Talk About Food*, the name came from "the Piedmontese add[ing] the sweet Italian suffix—ella to the American root 'nut.' Sweet sound, sweet taste."

Tabasco Sauce: Civil War epic

One has to wonder whether Edmund McIlhenny had a Scarlett O'Hara moment before he invented Tabasco Sauce. McIlhenny's route to the popular condiment was shaped by the Civil War in a tale nearly as epic as *Gone with the Wind*. Before the conflict between North and South, McIlhenny was a successful banker in New Orleans. And while he loved spicy foods, he probably gave little thought to the production of pepper sauces. But his destiny began taking shape in 1862 when the Union army entered the Queen City, forcing McIlhenny and his wife, Mary, to flee to Avery Island, a strange little piece of land jutting up from the Louisiana Marshes. Mary's family owned a plantation and salt mines there and the couple thought it would be a safe place to wait out the hostilities. Bad call. The Union army quickly comprehended that Avery Island's salt deposits were perfect for preserving meat for its soldiers. Not long after taking New Orleans, the northerners laid siege on Avery Island, capturing the salt mines and forcing the McIlhennys to flee again for their lives—this time to Texas.

When the war finally ended, Edmund and Mary made the arduous trip back to their plantation and just like Vivien Leigh's character on the big screen found nothing but devastation. The family mansion had been sacked and the crops plundered. But there was at least one edible that survived. During the Mexican-American war a business associate had supposedly given McIlhenny some capsicum peppers, an herb that is indigenous to Mexico. McIlhenny had planted a small crop on the plantation and given it little thought. Now it was one of the only things left to the family's name.

McIlhenny took the juicy peppers and seized the other commodity primarily at his disposal: the deposits of salt that still remained on the island. He threw in a little vinegar, poured the mixture into an old small cologne bottle and liked what he tasted. He initially wanted to call his stuff "Petite Anse Sauce," after Avery Island, which was also known as Petite Anse. When Mary's father balked at using the family property's name for such a venture, McIlhenny went for something a little more arbitrary: He dubbed it "E. McIlhenny Tabasco Pepper Sauce." Though there are conflicting reports on why he used *Tabasco*, it was likely taken from the title of a region in Mexico. Whatever the case, he simply liked the word.

McIlhenny, who undoubtedly never saw himself entering the condiments game before the war, started slowly with his new invention, initially putting together 350 two-ounce bottles. From the start, McIlhenny was a savvy marketer. So much so that at least one author claims some of his widely accepted story of success was borrowed from another New Orleans businessman to bolster his narrative. According to Jeffrey Rothfeder's Tabasco history, *McIlhenny's Gold*, an epicure named Maunsel White (who died the same year that the McIlhennys fled from Avery Island) actually received the original pepper seeds from a Mexican-American veteran, producing a pepper sauce that gave McIlhenny his inspiration to plant seeds following his return from Texas. Rothfeder also claims McIlhenny never used discarded cologne bottles for his original product.

Either way, Tabasco was undoubtedly an unintended product of Civil War looting and today enjoys sales of fifty million two-ounce units annually in America alone. All of which ensured that McIlhenny (and generations of his relatives to come) would never go hungry again.

Whipped Cream: Student's failed hypothesis

Have you ever tried to whip cream by hand? It's slow, arduous work. So there's little doubt that when Charles Getz invented an aerosol can that could instantly dispense sweet, fluffy, light cream, it put a smile on lots of faces (and not just dazed ones from wayward teens looking for a hit of the nitrous oxide used in the dispensers).

Although Getz had worked as a soda jerk and knew what a drag it was to manually whip cream, he never intended to save ice-cream sundae makers some hassles. It was the Depression and such an endeavor would have seemed frivolous. In 1931 Getz was a student at the University of Illinois, and like most college folk of the era (or any era for that matter) he needed to work to stay in school.

As a chemistry major, Getz was able to line up a part-time job at the college's Dairy Bacteriology Department. His goal in the gig was to come up with better ways to sterilize milk. Getz's best idea was to store milk using high gas pressure, which he believed would repel bacteria. He began running experiments and while his hypothesis proved a loser, it did offer an interesting by-product—nicely whipped milk.

Getz figured that whipped cream could be an excellent application for his discovery and, luckily, he had just the right professor to help encourage further development. Along with teaching analytic chemistry at the University of Illinois, G. Frederick Smith had established a small chemical company in 1928. Smith saw the practical applications for Getz's find and also had the infrastructure to nurture it.

A big early hurdle was coming up with the right gas to create the whipped cream. Most options left an unpleasant taste. After trial and error, Getz happened upon nitrous oxide—the odorless and (more important) tasteless gas used by dentists.

In April 1935 at the American Chemical Society, the pair unveiled their findings to much fanfare. Using a siphon bottle put under pressure, they were able to force carbon dioxide into cream, transforming it into the whipped variety in about a minute. The gadget also produced three times the volume compared with what hand-whipped efforts could offer. Wrote one enthralled journalist: "Yes, the chemists, who figure out the problems of war and industry and medicine … have even invaded the kitchen to solve the housewives' cares."

Named "Instantwhip," the new product was advertised as "Economical. Inexpensive. Convenient." Over time other brands would flood the market, leading to a slew of patent lawsuits. In a missed marketing opportunity, Instantwhip required users to refill their containers when empty. This opened the door for Reddi-wip, which gained a competitive advantage by offering disposable cans. Still, Getz's inadvertent discovery ushered in the aerosol age—leading to sprays for everything from hair products to cleaning solution. Not a bad resumé filler for a college kid just trying to pay his way through school.

Worcestershire Sauce: Forgotten barrel

John Lea and William Perrins knew how to keep a secret. In the mid-1800s, these chemists (British-speak for pharmacists) created one of the Victorian Era's most enduring condiments: Worcestershire (pronounced woos-TER-sheer) sauce. Beginning in 1837, Lea and Perrins convinced ship stewards to pack bottles on long voyages. The argument: Their sauce kept incredibly well and its strong, tangy flavor was particularly adept at covering up the taste of meats that spoiled during extensive journeys.

The sales pitch was a winner as the sauce sailed around the globe. It was used by gold miners in Northern California and sheep herders in New Zealand. The condiment even popped up in the forbidden city of Lhasa in Tibet. True to Lea and Perrins's word, the sauce did possess amazing resilience. Case in point: A Worcestershire bottle found on a boat shipwrecked in 1918 was still edible when discovered in 1989.

With such success, the inventors seriously safeguarded their formula. For years, Lea and Perrins were the only two who knew all the details necessary to manufacture the sauce. Even about 150 years after the condiment's invention only four people at the company's main plant in Worcester, England (about 125 miles northwest of London), knew the full roster of ingredients.

When it came to the origins of their sauce, the chemists also worked on a need-to-know basis. The bottles simply stated that it came from the "recipe of a nobleman in the county" of Worcestershire. From that, stories have been built. For years, executives who took over Lea and Perrins's company after their deaths embraced one anecdote starring a local military man named Lord Sandys. According to the tale, Lord Sandys had served as the governor of Bengal and upon returning to England wanted a curry similar to the kind he found in India. He approached the two plucky chemists, who strove diligently to do the lord's bidding. But much to their dismay, the men failed and placed a bin of their botched work in their cellar. Sometime later, looking to clean house, the pair planned to discard their woebegotten experiment when one of them (or a clerk) took a taste and found it very pleasing. The time spent fermenting in the cellar had turned the inedible into an indelible sauce.

It's a great story but one that's lacked the staying power of the actual product. In 1997 a company employee named Brian Keogh wrote *The Secret Sauce—A History of Lea & Perrins*. In the book, he pointed out that a Lord Sandys was never governor of Bengal and "as far as available records show, ever in India." This led one Lea & Perrins manager to concede, "We have had to say that the saga of Lord Sandys may not be God's own truth."

An 1884 edition of New Zealand paper the *Star* offered a plausible alternative. One day Elizabeth Caroline Grey, who was a prominent Worcestershire author, visited the lord's wife, Lady Sandys. The noblewoman commented that she longed for some good curry powder.

Mrs. Grey said she had a recipe, which her uncle, the former chief justice of India, had relayed to her. She recommended Lea and Perrins as excellent chemists who could produce a sauce from her uncle's instructions. Whether the chemists struggled is unclear. It is said that they originally made the sauce in 1835—some two years before selling it publicly. So the accidental element could have occurred. Still, as the tight-lipped Lea and Perrins are long gone, this is a secret that may never be revealed.

Drinks

Champagne: Devil's bubbly and a timely pilgrimage

If you've ever enjoyed a good bottle of champagne, you may believe it's more an act of nature than a drink. Just ask eighteenth-century nobles in Europe's royal courts. For them, the bubbly liquid was the tonic that propelled many an amorous tryst. France's Philippe II d'Orléans was a huge fan. "The orgies never started until everyone was in a state of joy that champagne brings," said one regular at the French palace when Philippe was in charge. Russia's Catherine the Great was also known to use the beverage to get her sexual conquests in the mood as well.

With the drink's ability to put people into an otherworldly state of mind, it probably makes sense that original sparkling wine was not invented by any human. But considering its properties, it may be surprising that it was initially uncovered as an unwanted by-product.

Originally known as the "devil's wine" (and not because of the fun it caused), the drink's carbonation sent vintners into mad fits—or worse. You see, the bubbles in sparkling wine were the product of fluctuations in the weather. Though winemakers didn't know it at the time, vino begins to ferment during mild weather and then stops if the weather gets too cold during the winter months. In those situations a second fermentation occurs when warm days return. This double fermentation creates a build-up of carbonation.

The results were both physically and economically dangerous. Many winemakers wouldn't go down into their cellars unless they were wearing an iron mask as the fear of bottles suddenly bursting was legitimate. (At one winery, three men lost eyes thanks to glass explosions.) Financially, the situation wasn't any better. One firm started a season with 6,000 bottles only to end it with 120. In the northern Champagne region, where only their sparkling wine can be called by the famed name today, particularly cold winters followed by a second fermentation in the spring led to a great number of these bubbly explosions.

It was so bad that most were flabbergasted by these occurrences. "These phenomena are so strange . . . that no one will ever be able to explain them," one scientist said. "All these accidents are so varied and extraordinary that even the most experienced professional cannot foresee them or prevent them from happening."

A monk helped prove that man of science wrong. Pierre Pérignon came from a well-to-do family and could have followed his father into the civil service. Instead, he felt a religious calling and became a Benedictine monk. In 1668, at the age of thirty, Dom Pérignon (as he became known) took responsi-

bility for business affairs at the Abbey of Hautvillers. Located in Champagne, Hautvillers made wine, which had once been the toast of France. But because of poorly maintained grounds, competition from elsewhere in the country, and exploding bottles, the business was in serious financial jeopardy.

Pérignon, who would oversee the cellar until 1715, turned the venture around by applying exacting standards for all its wines—sparkling or otherwise. Many incorrectly credit Pérignon with inventing champagne. In reality he fought to keep bubbles out of his wine. Claude Möet probably deserves the most credit for creating a broad champagne market and others also played key roles in corralling the bubbles. But one essential innovation that Pérignon did bring to the area's famed bubbly was the cork.

One day, two Spanish monks came to stay at Hautvillers on their way to Sweden. Pérignon noticed the unique stoppers in their water jugs and asked about them. They were from the bark of trees that grew in Catalonia and proved a great way to seal bottles. Before then Pérignon was using wood pegs covered in hemp soaked in olive oil. While many historians point out that cork stoppers had been around before, Pérignon's cork introduction to champagne—along with the creation of thicker bottles innovated in Great Britain—proved essential in holding back the carbonation, keeping not only royals but us regular people effervescent ever since.

Coca-Cola: Headaches and prohibition

America was in need of healing following the Civil War, and one of the unlikeliest medicines to come out of the reconstruction years was Coca-Cola. Today, we know it by its corporate ingredients—one part soft drink and one part marketing juggernaut—but back in the late nineteenth century Coca-Cola was created as a "nerve tonic" with the purpose of remedying such maladies as depression, hysteria, anxiety, and indigestion.

The drink's inventor, John Pemberton, probably knew a lot about the post-traumatic stress caused by the war. He'd been a cavalry officer in the Confederate army. A well-respected pharmacist by trade, he settled in Atlanta following the hostilities and began producing patent medicines. Like so many others, he was looking to make a buck by developing problem-solving products for just about any ill. "Someone in need of a hair-straightening ointment or a remedy for a cough that refused to go away might have purchased one of Pemberton's products," wrote Constance L. Hays in her book *The Real Thing: Truth and Power at the Coca-Cola Company*.

It was in this snake-oil-salesman environment that Pemberton created his secret formula for Coca-Cola in 1886. The early drink did have coca leaf extract (street name: cocaine) along with caffeine from cola nuts and heaps of sugar. Back then the narcotic was legally utilized in many goods. In truth, a syrupy elixir for all ages wasn't his initial plan. At first Pemberton rolled out a drink called French Wine Cocoa, which had many of the same ingredients as his sweet family-friendly classic but with a major difference: It featured alcohol. Combining the ups of sugar, caffeine, and Colombian marching powder with a boozy downer produced a beverage that sold well in the southeast. But when Atlanta decreed a prohibition on alcohol in 1886, he was forced to innovate a softer drink.

One story that's a myth: the addition of carbonated water was an accident. In reality, sparkling water had been around for about seventy years before Pemberton's invention—and was regularly utilized in the making of many of these tonics. Some even believed that fizzy water could cure shingles.

So did the original Coca-Cola really have a healing value? The man who initially built Coke into a massive brand, Asa Candler, was allegedly convinced of it. As a child, he'd fallen out of a horse-drawn carriage, an accident that left him with migraine headaches. He found that Coca-Cola erased the pain. Candler was so impressed that he purchased the formula and the rights to sell the drink from Pemberton not long after its invention.

Candler would continue to push it as a vitality-restoring wonder in the early going. "The medical properties of the Coca Plant and the extract of the celebrated African Cola Nut make it a medical preparation of great value, which the best physicians unhesitatingly endorse and recommend for mental and physical exhaustion, headache, tired feeling, mental depression, etc.," he wrote to a Georgia doctor in an 1890 Coca-Cola sales pitch.

If it did have restorative properties, we wouldn't know today because while many of the original ingredients remain, cocaine, as we're all aware, is not one of them. By the beginning of the twentieth century, narcotics were a no-go for drinks and Candler removed the drug, advertising the modification throughout the country. (Some say a minute amount of cocaine remained in the formula until the 1920s.) The decision to distance the drink from the drug was a good move as attitudes had absolutely changed. Instead of referring to Coke as a medicine, many in the South for the first few decades of the 1900s remembered its drug lineage, giving the drink a different nickname: dope.

Coffee: Dancing goats

Before there were perky baristas and skim latte lovers, there were goats. Yes, coffee's pioneers were those cloven-hoofed beasts and if they could talk they would have likely asked for double-caf hold the liquid.

The most pervasive explanation of coffee's beginnings takes us to Ethiopia circa AD 850, where a humble goatherd named Kaldi was having headaches with his flock. Kaldi, who would cover great ground with his animals, found himself in a slightly new area one day. The goats grazed on bushes full of red-cherry-looking local beans. Clearly, Kaldi had no idea that centuries later these beans would make Starbucks billions. He was just concerned when the evening came and his goats were practically dancing around instead of taking a rest. (This probably shouldn't be surprising as studies have shown that a single cup of coffee two hours before bedtime can more than double the time it takes for an average adult to fall asleep; one can only imagine what gnawing on the actual beans did to these four-legged friends.)

Perplexed by his flock's late-night activity, Kaldi showed the beans to either (depending who you believe) members of a local monastery or a group of traveling monks, who were resting in the same area.

Whomever he gave the berries to, they loved their pick-me-up qualities and began experimenting, leading to the invention of coffee.

Like most of these early tales, it's hard to know where truth and myth diverge. It's safe to say that religious figures, like those in Kaldi's story, played a role in the spread of the drink. Priests and monks found that coffee's properties helped keep them sharp during long religious ceremonies. Moreover, coffee emerged as a popular drink in the Islamic world, where stimulating alcoholic drinks were banned.

The first written mention of coffee as a drink came from an Arabic physician named Rhazes in the tenth century. The drink's popularity picked up in the thirteenth century when farmers in Yemen began cultivating the beans, roasting them, and giving the brew the name *Qahwah* (or *Kahweh*), an old Arabic term for wine.

If dancing goats are a bit too much to take, there is another accidental coffee story that is on far more solid ground. Well, in reality, it is far more about the ocean than solid ground. Ludwig Roselius was a successful German coffee magnate, buying beans from around the world. In 1903, he received some bad news: A shipment from Latin America had gotten waterlogged on its long voyage.

Instead of throwing out the soaked beans, Roselius directed his researchers to conduct experiments to consider the salt water's impact. Much to everyone's surprise between the salt water and a process of pressurized steaming to extract the brine, nearly all of the caffeine was removed from the beans. Based on that discovery (plus other break throughs using solvents), Roselius brought the first decaffeinated coffee to market. Sanka, which was named after the French combination of *sans* and *caffeine*, was introduced to the American market in 1923, leaving people and goats alike in the United States an option for a hot drink before a good night's sleep.

Cognac: Savvy Dutch merchants

For many, the only type of brandy that will do is cognac. Both Napoleon Bonaparte and Winston Churchill were believers in its superior quality. Made in France's Charente region, cognac was also the civilized drink of choice when it came time for opposing leaders to toast the armistice following the peace treaty signing that ended World War I.

As sophisticated as it may be—and as much as some might call its creation an art form—the birth of cognac can be directly attributed to a lucky business decision made by some of the most adroit traders centuries ago.

The concept of distilling alcohol is one that dates back to antiquity. The Moors are widely acknowledged as having developed the process in the seventh and eighth centuries. As devout Muslims, they weren't much for partying. Instead, they used their stills to produce medicinal spirits and perfumes.

Nevertheless, distilling became known throughout Europe and could be called upon to brew up some hard-drinking concoctions. Here's where the Dutch join the story and unwittingly helped elevate the process to a rarefied level.

Dutch merchants were among the most successful traders in the sixteenth century. Their game plan included encouraging local suppliers to focus on a single crop, helping those producers with techniques to improve yields and offering fair terms for purchase. When it came to wine, they knew where to go: Bordeaux. This region of France was a premier spot to purchase what was an essential commodity throughout the world.

As much as they were helpful partners, the Dutch traders were also realists. The wine in Bordeaux was good, but local government charged pricey tariffs for shipping the drink out of its port. The Dutch probably crunched the numbers and decided to move on. They went about sixty miles north to Charente and centered their wine trade on the town of Cognac. It didn't matter that wine produced in this area was considered pretty awful. It was cheap and the local port was duty free. There was also the benefit of large local salt deposits, which offered another commodity to load onto their ships.

The next obstacle the Dutch faced was maximizing their haul. Again, they had an answer. Rather than loading excessive barrels of wine, they would cut down on the volume of the vino. Their plan was simple: burn off (or distill) water from the wine, leaving less liquid to store on board. As wine typically didn't travel well, this would have the added bonus of keeping the already subpar alcohol fresher on the voyage.

At first, they planned to reintroduce water to the concentrated alcohol when they arrived at their destinations, but the merchants shifted gears after tasting the condensed spirit. It was far better than the cheap wine. The Dutch called the new product *brandewijn* or "burnt wine." The English, who were regular buyers of Dutch goods, anglicized the moniker to "brandy wine" and in the end called it "brandy."

Within the next century, a second key component to cognac's development occurred: the introduction of double distillation, which smoothed out the drink's flavor while keeping the alcohol content high. Charente lore attributes double distillation to a knight named Jacques de la Croix Maron. Returning from a crusade in the first half of the 1600s, the knight found his wife in bed with a neighbor and killed them both. Apparently, that was okay with the local folk, but it did trouble the knight's conscience (you don't say?). He began having a reoccurring dream that he was burned alive twice in Hell. The knight decided that he needed to burn something that he loved twice in order to rid himself of his guilt. He chose his beloved wine and the result was the double-distilled cognac. Personally, I'm not betting on this story's veracity. Couldn't he have come up with something a little more precious? And why did the knight end up on top following a double homicide?

In actuality, double distillation was probably the invention of a smart businessman who was looking for a competitive advantage. As for the Dutch, they continued to make sharp moves with the liquor. In 1652 they purchased a large swath of land on the Cape of Good Hope, including what would become Cape Town, for some Virginian tobacco and a few barrels of cognac.

Gibson Martini: Wry bartender, ingenious diplomat, or San Francisco pride

The Gibson martini is an incredibly minor variation on a theme. It gets a special name, even though it's essentially a standard martini with one notable exception—instead of an olive or lemon peel garnish, a pickled pearl onion or two is used. (Sorry to hardcore Gibson boosters; I realize you may recoil at that assessment.)

If you do love the onion, you're probably drinking the Gibson because one tastemaking man was a bit bored at a bar one evening. Charles Dana Gibson was an illustrator and arbiter of chic in the late nineteenth and early twentieth century. His Gibson Girl sketches of an attractive statuesque woman, which appeared in such trendsetting magazines as *Life* and *Harper's,* were considered the feminine ideal of the time.

Along with drawing fine women, Gibson also liked the finer things in life. To that end, he was a regular patron of The Players, a New York club for the ultra cool in Gibson's day. At the time of Gibson's great fame, the man behind the bar was Charles Connolly. Not one to be star-struck, the Irish-born Connolly had served as a confidant for a broad spectrum of luminaries from the great satirist Mark Twain to the esteemed actor John Barrymore. He was congenial, gregarious, and known for his warm smile so it makes sense that Gibson also had an affinity for him.

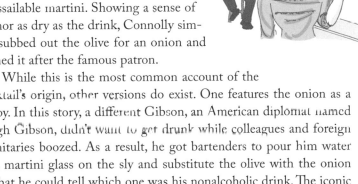

One day Gibson came into The Players, saddled up to the bar, and was keen for something out of the ordinary. Chatting up Connolly, Gibson challenged the barkeep to improve upon the already unassailable martini. Showing a sense of humor as dry as the drink, Connolly simply subbed out the olive for an onion and named it after the famous patron.

While this is the most common account of the cocktail's origin, other versions do exist. One features the onion as a decoy. In this story, a different Gibson, an American diplomat named Hugh Gibson, didn't want to get drunk while colleagues and foreign dignitaries boozed. As a result, he got bartenders to pour him water in a martini glass on the sly and substitute the olive with the onion so that he could tell which one was his nonalcoholic drink. The iconic *Joy of Cooking* said Gibson pulled the stunt because he "found himself obliged to attend a stupefying number of cocktail parties." Most martini-ologists believe this is a tall tale.

Then there's a San Francisco fellow named Walter D. K. Gibson, who has received tribute for the drink's invention by a number of Bay

Area writers. There is evidence to support that this Gibson did invent an eponymous cocktail, but it's worth noting that even if this West Coast Gibson came first (Walter apparently came up with his drink in the 1890s), it didn't include the all-important onion.

All this points back to Charles Dana Gibson, whose fame likely led to the spread of Connolly's onion-inspired work. One would think that only the clout of a man like the illustrator Gibson could have turned such a small substitution into a world-renowned drink.

Irish Coffee: Dangerous flight

Joe Sheridan kept it simple when he applied for a job in 1943 at the Foynes Flying Boat Base near Shannon, Ireland. "Dear Sir," the application letter went, "I'm the man for the job. Yours sincerely, Joe Sheridan." He didn't know just how right he was. Within no time, Sheridan, who amazingly did get the position, would capitalize on a blustery evening to create one of St. Patrick's Day's most popular libations—the Irish coffee.

Sheridan's new job was working at the cafe on base. But this was no ordinary bar and restaurant.

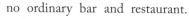

Although Ireland was officially neutral during World War II, the country clandestinely ferried high-level Allied VIPs and military personnel on long-haul flights from Europe to a number of locations, including the United States and Canada. Between German fighters and inclement weather, this was not an easy run. Winston Churchill once flew out of Foynes during the war and nearly had to make an emergency sea landing because of a particularly grueling storm.

It was a night similar to the one Churchill faced that led Sheridan to his delicious and bracing combination of Power's Irish Whiskey, coffee, sugar, and a dollop of cream on top. Late one winter night in 1943, a plane set out from Foynes to Botwood, Newfoundland, but ran into bad weather. By one account the flight was five hours into its journey when it was forced to turn around and return to the air base. The pilot alerted the Foynes control tower and staff was asked to come back to cater to the passengers who would undoubtedly be weary from ten hours of flying.

Sheridan knew he'd have to come up with something special on the fly for the returning travelers. Although whiskey in tea was a common Irish combination, the chef figured these passengers—primarily North Americans—would rather have a concoction featuring coffee (more popular in the New World) with the alcohol. When the waylaid fliers got a taste of the new drink, one reportedly asked Sheridan if the soothing cup of joe was Brazilian coffee. Sheridan responded that it was Irish coffee and the name stuck.

Recognizing he'd hit upon something special, Sheridan spent the next few weeks working on his new drink. Showing a marketer's touch, he came up with the idea of serving his Irish coffee in a fancy stemmed glass. When the Foynes base closed in 1945, Sheridan moved along with other members of the catering staff to a new airport across the river, which today is known as Shannon International Airport. He continued serving his Irish coffee to the civilians who now used this airport as a trans-Atlantic hub. By 1947 Sheridan's coffee was chosen as the airport's "official welcoming beverage," and a few years later, one particularly proactive passenger would become besotted with the drink. His name was Stanton Delaplane, a fancy-dressing Pulitzer Prize–winning travel writer from San Francisco.

Upon returning home, Delaplane went to his favorite watering hole, The Buena Vista. Sidling up to the bar, he told the establishment's owner Jack Koeppler about Irish coffee. Koeppler loved the concept and on November 10, 1952, the pair spent a long evening trying to re-create the drink. Alas, an exact imitation eluded them for two reasons: They couldn't get the coffee/whiskey taste just right and the cream kept sinking. Koeppler developed an obsession, making a pilgrimage to Shannon Airport to get the correct recipe directly from Sheridan. According to The Buena Vista's website, Koeppler would return with the perfect whiskey for the job but continued to struggle with the cream. Finally, Koeppler went to George Christopher, a dairy owner who would go on to be San Francisco's thirty-fourth mayor. Christopher helped devise a cream—aged for forty-eight hours and frothed to exacting consistency—that could float atop the drink. According to the Foynes Flying Boat Museum, Sheridan would later immigrate to the United States and continue serving his Irish coffee until his death in 1962. That he never stopped dispensing his signature drink shouldn't be surprising. Clearly, he was the best man for that job.

Kool-Aid: Post office complications

A borderline obsession with Jell-O and limitations with the US Postal Service led Edwin E. Perkins to create one of the United States' most iconic drink mixes—Kool-Aid. Perkins's story is also one that truly reflects the time and spirit of America in the early twentieth century.

Perkins was born in 1889 in Lewis, Iowa, to a family that had moved west to seek a better way of life. One of ten children, Perkins and his family ultimately ended up in Fumas County, Nebraska, where they cultivated a farm. Although those were rough times in Nebraska, the Perkins family survived and even flourished thanks in large part to a strong work ethic. In fact, they prospered enough that by the time Edwin Perkins was eleven years old, his father was running a successful general store in the tiny hamlet of Hendley, Nebraska. The young Perkins would work as a clerk at the shop and while helping out, he was introduced to an innovative dessert that was sweeping the nation—Jell-O. Perkins was smitten with its brightly colored packaging and easy-to-produce process.

The wobbly gelatin inspired the young man to channel his inner entrepreneur. Within a year or two of his wiggly, jiggly discovery, he was experimenting with a chemistry set. The goal: Concoct his own product that would win the love of the masses. He also began a number of other cottage industries, including publishing a weekly newspaper, the *Hendley Delphic*, and working as the village postmaster.

The postmaster gig was a good one for Perkins because along with everything else, he'd established a mail-order business. As a teenager, he was hawking everything from perfumes to something called Nix-O-Tine Tobacco Remedy, which was an antismoking kit. Still, he never lost sight of trying to reach the heights of Jell-O glory.

In the early 1920s, Perkins thought he'd found it. Although he was now manufacturing more than 125 different "household products," ranging from face creams and lotions to salves and soaps, his most popular product was something called Fruit Smack. Like Jell-O, there were six flavors, but it wasn't something you needed to let set. Instead, it was a liquid concentrate that could be poured into water to create a pitcher of a sweet drink for mere pennies.

Alas, his expected gold mine was running into a consistent problem. Units of Fruit-Smack were shipped in small four-ounce corked glass bottles and packages kept getting returned because during the bustle of shipping, the vials were cracking and leaking. Throw in the cost of the heavy containers cutting into profits, and Perkins had no choice but to come up with an alternative.

Again, Jell-O was the perfect model. A dry mix, Jell-O kept easily and, even more important, could be safely shipped in paper packaging. Perkins became determined to devise a dehydrated concentrate form of his Fruit-Smack that could sidestep his shipping problems. It took a while, but by 1927 he cracked it, offering, naturally, six flavors: raspberry, cherry, grape, lemon, orange, and root-beer. Ironically, despite the inspiration for the Kool-Aid mix (avoiding packaging issues), Perkins had problems devising the perfect materials to ship his new powder mix. In the end a brightly colored envelope—a la Jell-O—with a soft waxed paper lining worked perfectly. Before long he had a product that even Jell-O makers would envy. By 1950, he was shipping a whopping 323 million packets annually.

Ovaltine: Foul-tasting health drink

If Ovaltine's long-departed inventor Dr. Georg Wander were around today, he would surely be confused by the fact that when people consider his drink they likely picture a comfortable little child warming up with a late-night combination of his mix and milk before dozing off to sleep.

Wander had far different, more altruistic intentions for his invention. In the second half of the nineteenth century, the Swiss chemist was very concerned about people's diets. At the time so many individuals suffered from nutritional deficiencies. In particular he worried about children, the infirm, the weak, and even breastfeeding women. Wander pledged himself to coming up with a product that could serve as a "nourishing food supplement."

As the basis for his new blend, he chose barley malt. Though best known for its role in brewing beer, it had been lauded for its medicinal values for some 2,000 years. Wander developed an inexpensive way to produce malt extract and then fortified it with nutritious things like vitamin D and phosphorous. Wander must have figured he had come up with a valuable way to fight malnutrition.

But his original syrupy mix had a major glitch. Quite simply, even the malnourished want something that tastes good, and the healthy (but bitter) malt invention wasn't meeting that need. After Wander's death in 1897, his son Albert took over the family business. The younger Wander recognized what his father had missed. Along with figuring out a way to make a dry powder, he added such ingredients as sugar, eggs, and cocoa to round out the drink's flavor. In 1904 Albert unveiled Ovomaltine (named for the combination of the Latin word for egg—*ovo*—and malt).

Albert had a different view of the drink's value than his father. Wrote one journalist, "[H]e marketed it as an energy drink—the Red Bull of its day, as it were." Within a few years of its debut, Albert truncated the name of the mix to Ovaltine and began shipping it abroad. When clever marketers in Britain got ahold of it, they started selling the product directly to the youth set as a healthy hot cocoa alternative. Relying heavily on radio advertising, Ovaltine execs sponsored a show called The League of Ovaltineys. It featured a secret society of kids who would give away badges and other goodies to listeners. The Ovaltineys lured audiences as large as five million children, who were expected to follow the group's code. The rules included the wonderfully self-serving declaration: "Every day [I must] . . . drink my delicious Ovaltine, to make me fit and happy, with a mind that's bright and keen." The approach was so profitable that when Ovaltine reached the United States similar tactics were employed with the company underwriting such popular radio shows as *Little Orphan Annie* and *Captain Midnight*.

While it wasn't Wander's goal or intention to create a good old-fashioned comfort drink, he should rest easy knowing that even today it remains a wholesome option. While the brand has lost its zip in the marketplace, Ovaltine still offers a healthy combination of vitamins A, C, D, B1, B2, and B6 along with niacin and phosphorous.

Pink Lemonade: Accidental carnival creation

The circus is all about hyperbole. Come see the tallest she-man in the world! Watch a blindfolded diver plummet one thousand feet into a goldfish bowl! There is always a fantastic saga to be told. The origins of pink lemonade, which everyone seems to agree was created by circus folk, is no exception. The only question is which mythic yarn you want to believe.

Lion tamer extraordinaire George Conklin offered the most detailed explanation of the drink's beginnings in his 1921 memoir *The Ways of the Circus: Being the Memories and Adventures of George Conklin Tamer of Lions*. He claimed his brother, Pete Conklin, made the first brew in 1857. At the time Pete was working with the Jerry Mabie show, which was like working on the biggest touring rock concert today. Mabie's circus held a record, according to George, for going from town-to-town nonstop for *seven years*.

Unfortunately, Pete would have a disagreement with Mabie over wages and quit the show. But as his brother would write, "Pete was a youngster and didn't mind taking long chances." That iffy prospect came in the form of doing concessions. He used his savings to purchase a couple of mules, a covered wagon, and some stock: peanuts, sugar, tartaric acid, and a lemon. According to George, Pete called the lemon "the best example of a friend I ever met."

With his goods, he'd set up outside the big top and focus on selling old-fashioned yellow-tinged lemonade. The color change came one day when business was so great Pete ran out of water. "There were no wells or springs near," George explained. "He rushed all around the show for water, but could find none." Desperate, Pete sprinted into the dressing tent and came across Fannie Jamieson, one of the show's bareback riders. She had just cleaned her pink tights in a vat of water, leaving the liquid looking a deep pink hue.

"Without giving any explanation or stopping to answer her questions, Pete grabbed the tub of pink water and ran," George said. "It took only a minute to throw in some of the tartaric acid and the pieces of the . . . lemon and then he began to call out, 'Come quickly, buy some fine strawberry lemonade.'"

The new-look lemonade did double the business of ordinary refreshment and, allegedly, ushered in a new style of the drink. So did Pete or future lemonade peddlers immediately change the formula to avoid icky additives for the pink coloring? Not really, claimed George, who said that subsequent water was procured "with no particular squeamishness regarding its source" and that "enough aniline dye [was added] to give it a rich pink" appearance.

Despite George Conklin's detail, there is another simpler (slightly more hygienic) story explaining the beginnings of the colorful drink. It comes from a shady fellow named Henry E. Allott (alias Bunk Allen; personally, any guy with an alias makes me nervous). Allott was a Chicago saloonkeeper and gambler who had more than one run-in with the law. He was also a circus promoter and when he died in 1912, a number of newspapers, including the *New York Times*, credited Henry/Bunk with coming up with pink lemonade as a teenager. "One day while mixing a tub full of the orthodox yellow kind he dropped some red cinnamon candies in by mistake," the *New York Times* wrote. "The resulting rose-tinted mixture sold so surprisingly well that he continued to dispense his chance discovery."

According to research done by Lynne Olver, who runs the encyclopedic Internet website www.foodtimeline.org, this story, if true, would mean Allott invented the drink around 1872–1873—long after Conklin's claimed invention. Moreover, one wonders how Allott got his newly colored drink tasting like lemonade instead of cinnamon. Then again, considering Pete Conklin's story, I don't think I'd even want to know.

Tea (and Iced Tea): Mystic brew

In many Asian cultures, tea is more than a soothing drink to curl up with on a frigid day. It has spiritual significance. Some early Chinese texts referred to the drink as an ingredient in the fabled brew known as the elixir of immortality. When it spread to Japan by the ninth century, it was used as a ritual drink. Even today, tea ceremonies are a serious affair often linked to following a Zen path.

Truth be told, the real origin of the first cup of tea is likely lost in time. But its mystical quality has naturally led to a legend that many cling tightly to. The lead character of the story is a great ancient cultural figure named Emperor Shen Nung (or Shennong). Renowned as a fantastic scholar and a deft herbalist who tasted scores of herbs to determine their value, Shen Nung was more than just a ruler. To that end, his name's English translation is "divine farmer."

Tea's seminal moment is pinpointed to 2737 BC. Shen Nung was very concerned about hygiene and often drank boiled water to burn off impurities. One day he was making a pot of the liquid under a tea tree when a light breeze blew some of the leaves into the cauldron. Keeping with his reputation as a person willing to try all types of foliage, he took a sip and was moved by its taste and stimulating kick (hello, caffeine).

There is absolutely no way to confirm or deny this story. It's even unclear whether Shen Nung existed or is a legendary figure himself. Many scholars feel confident that the drink was likely around at the time that Shen Nung allegedly lived, but it wasn't until the third century BC that tea even makes it into writing. In that text a Chinese doctor recommended it for "increasing concentration and alertness."

While not nearly as dramatic, the iced type of tea also has its own origins myth. This one takes place in 1904 at the St. Louis World's Fair. One of the vendors at the event was the India Tea Association, which, of course, sold steaming brewed tea. But much to the concessionaire's chagrin, during the sweltering summer, nobody at the fair had any interest in the hot drink. So Richard Blechynden, a special commissioner for the association, dispatched one of his waiters to get some ice and iced tea was born. This story received enough traction that in 1949, the *St. Louis Post-Dispatch* wrote all about the forty-fifth anniversary of iced tea's invention.

Unlike the uncertain beginnings of tea, Blechynden's moment of extemporaneous inspiration almost certainly didn't start us down the path to Snapple. Blechynden was at the 1904 fair, but a number of other vendors also served iced tea at the event as well. As menus were generally printed before the start of the proceedings, it's likely that all these other merchants, which included folks from such extremely different locales as Japan and Louisiana, were already serving it up well before Blechynden's purported moment of creation. In reality, according to research from author Pamela J. Vaccaro, iced tea was already a popular drink in many pockets of the United States at least two decades before the Fair.

White Zinfandel: Lucky fermentation

Once described as the "*TV Guide* of wines," White Zinfandel, the sweet pink wine that can be picked up at the corner store for cheap, has often been derided by serious connoisseurs. Those wine snobs will be even more frustrated to know that White Zin would have never been if not for a combination of a nosy wine buyer and a fluke of nature.

The drink's genesis dates back to 1972 at the Napa Valley, California, winery Sutter Homes Vineyard. The Red Zinfandel grape is used in making a dry red vino; that season the vineyard's winemaker Bob Trinchero decided to remove some of the juices from the grape in order to create a more concentrated vintage. As part of the process, Trinchero was left with 550 gallons of white juice that he figured might be usable in making Chablis. Enter Darrell Corti, a legendary wine retailer from Sacramento. He said he'd buy half of the cases made from the juice if Trinchero would bottle it. Corti, whose expertise would later earn him induction into the Vintner's Hall of Fame, suggested that the new wine be called *Oeil de Perdrix* (French for "eye of the partridge"). Trinchero's response, "Oh, okay. I can't pronounce it." He made up the labels anyway and sent it in to the Bureau of Alcohol, Tobacco, and Firearms.

Yes, along with fighting bad guys and making sure that contraband cigarettes don't flood the black market, the ATF is responsible for wine naming. Apparently they take the job seriously as they told Trinchero he had to come up with an English description for the new wine. Although there is no such thing as a White Zinfandel grape, he combined the color of the juice and the name of the grape, calling it "A White Zinfandel wine."

Even with Corti's intervention, the wine would have likely come and gone if not for a bit of luck. In 1973 Sutter Homes started selling small quantities of the drink, which at the time was a dry white. "I was thinking Chardonnay when I was making it," said Trinchero in an oral history he did for the University of California, Berkeley's Bancroft Library. But two years later, while making a vintage, a process known as "stuck fermentation" occurred. Basically, the fermentation process unintentionally stopped, leaving some residual sugar in the wine and giving it a completely different look and taste.

At first Trinchero was less than thrilled. "Oh, my God, it's got a pink tinge to it and it's too sweet," he recounted. "'What am I going to do now, because my customer is used to the dry, white one.' Then I said, 'The heck with it. I'm going to bottle it anyway.' Well, I had to. I couldn't do anything with four hundred cases; that was too much wine for me at the time."

It was a great call. In 1980 he bottled 24,000 cases; by 1995 the winery was churning out three million cases. In 2010 White Zinfandel represented 8 percent of all California wine shipments. "It's been an amazing story," he once quipped to *Wines & Vines* magazine. "I'm just glad it happened to me."

Kitchen Inventions and Innovations

Cellophane: Stained tablecloth

Cellophane was one of the twentieth century's biggest breakthroughs in food packaging. It replaced wax paper as the prime way to keep your sandwich—or really any food—fresh longer. It even changed the way the food industry worked, lessening the need for locally harvested goods. But the day its inventor, Jacques Brandenberger, first began his journey toward the product's invention, he wasn't thinking food—he had wine on his mind.

Brandenberger, a Swiss engineer, was sitting in a fine restaurant in Paris enjoying a meal when he saw another patron clumsily knock over a glass of red wine onto his table. The tablecloth was ruined and waiters scurried around quickly replacing the soiled sheet. Brandenberger concluded that a treated tablecloth that could wick away liquid would be a fantastic creation. The scientist immediately went to work on the idea.

He applied himself mightily in his quest. After some failures, he decided to try cellulose as the basis for a treatment. Made from the sugar molecules that comprise plant cell walls, cellulose was discovered in the late nineteenth century and was being used to make synthetic fibers like rayon. As cellulose is a resilient substance (it's the reason tree trunks and branches are so tough), an optimistic Brandenberger sprayed a dissolved form on a sheet.

The result initially looked like another letdown. The cloth came out stiff as a board, making it impossible to fold or put over a table. Luckily, Brandenberger noticed something interesting about this miscue: He could peel off the cellulose. This new clear sheet had some promising properties—while it wasn't impermeable to water, with some modifications, it became resistant to oils and grease and was flame resistant. Brandenberger still wasn't contemplating food at this point, but he did abandon his tablecloth dream and began working with his new substance. In 1908 he patented the viscose sheet, dubbing it cellophane (a shortening of *cellulose* to "cello" and adding "phane" from the Greek word *diaphanis*, meaning transparent). Early applications included using the material to wrap fancy French perfume bottles and even producing eye lenses for gas masks.

In 1923 Brandenberger licensed the US rights to his product to the famed chemical company DuPont. It was a DuPont scientist named William Hale Charch who came up with a way to make cellophane food friendly. His secret was adding a waterproof component. With Charch's tweak, perishables wouldn't get soggy from outside contaminants and safety was increased by preventing meat juices from soaking through packaging—a problem that often spread dangerous bacteria.

How cool was cellophane at the time? Composer Cole Porter, who was a rock star in his day, included it in his hit song "You're the Top." Porter called out cellophane alongside such top-notch wonders as the Leaning Tower of Pisa, Mona Lisa's smile, Mahatma Gandhi, and Napoleon Brandy. Proving that you shouldn't scrutinize lyrics too closely, the verse went "You're the National Gallery, you're Garbo's salary, you're cellophane." If you don't think the thin film was worthy of such high praise (Garbo did make a lot back then), consider this: Along with its role in food storage, cellophane also inspired Sellotape (otherwise known as Scotch Tape) when a 3M engineer figured out a way to add adhesive to Brandenberger's accidental discovery. But even if you disagree with Porter, it's safe to say cellophane's various uses sure beat a stain-fighting tablecloth.

CorningWare: Nuclear warheads

S. Donald Stookey was one of the biggest superstars in twentieth-century American science. His name appears on more than sixty patents and, in 1986, he received the National Medal of Technology from President Ronald Reagan for his uncanny ability to turn ideas into practical uses. He was so good that at one point during his career he decided he was tapped out of ideas and told executives at Corning, where he worked, that he planned to resign. Not wanting to lose Stookey, his bosses kept him on board by giving him a year off and an all-expenses-paid vacation around the world.

Yet, for all his talent, Stookey's most famous discovery—CorningWare—was the product of nothing more than mistakes on a bad day in 1952. Stookey was working with a plate of photosensitive glass that he planned to heat up to 600°C. For some reason (maybe he was distracted) he didn't keep a close eye on the experiment. When he returned to the furnace the temperature had risen to 900°C.

Stookey assumed he'd melted the glass and broken equipment. "I figured I had ruined the furnace," he said in a 1986 interview. But he was astounded to see the glass was intact when he opened the oven. It just had a new white color to it.

He quickly got a pair of tongs to pull it out, but he bungled the pickup and the glass tumbled to the floor. Much to Stookey's amazement, rather than breaking into a thousand pieces, it bounced around. "[I]t sounded like a piece of steel bouncing, so I figured something different must have happened," he said.

Stookey had created a form of ceramic glass, dubbed Pyroceram, that seemed like something out of a comic book. It could be heated and cooled to mind-numbing temperatures and still keep its shape while neither rusting nor eroding.

While Corning historically had much success with ovenware—the company introduced Pyrex in 1915—Stookey's invention was initially slated for another use. It was the height of the Cold War and improving the country's ballistic missile arsenal was more important than coming up with a foolproof casserole dish. As a result, the Pyroceram was used in making noses for nuclear warheads. In 1958, Corning realized that there was enough of the glass to go around and began selling the ultra-strong material under the CorningWare imprimatur. They embossed the white dishes with what became its iconic blue cornflower. (Geek note: Cornflowers were apparently chosen because men in love in olden days supposedly wore them; in the 1950s one hopes that this didn't mean that a good man purchased CorningWare as a show of amore.)

CorningWare was a wild hit as an indispensable kitchen item. Ads depicting food being cooked under extreme heat in one half of the cookware and, at the same time, being frozen on the other side successfully wooed customers. CorningWare's success spurred a sales jump from $25 million when Stookey joined the company in 1940 to $1.7 billion near the end of his career in 1985. That kind of income could have surely sent Stookey on a few more around-the-world vacations.

Dishwashers: Klutzy maids

It may seem like one of the most obvious questions and answers. Question: Why would somebody invent a dishwasher? Answer: To clean dishes, stupid! In truth, you would be far from stupid if you thought cleanliness wasn't the primary inspiration for the first commercially viable dishwasher.

At first glance Josephine Garis Cochrane would be an unlikely inventor. Cochrane was the wife of a wealthy Illinois politician when she decided to construct her earth-changing invention. As for her plates, cutlery, and glasses, there is nothing to suggest she wasn't just fine with their cleanliness after they were hand washed. That said, Josephine did have a problem—the kind of problem only a rich woman might have.

Her issue was that the servants in the Cochrane's 1880s household could get a little clumsy during washing. Increasingly, her beautiful china, some of which supposedly dated back to the seventeenth century, was getting chipped or (gasp) breaking in the hands of the help. She tried scrubbing them herself, but it was too much for her dainty disposition. So one day she stormed into the woodshed adjoining her stately home, rolled up her sleeves, and decided that no maid would ever damage her plates again!

At almost the same time, life would get a whole lot tougher for Mrs. Cochrane. Her husband William was sick when she resolved to make her contraption and died soon after. The tragedy gave her a more compelling reason than unchipped tea cups—let's call it livelihood—to succeed. Still, her husband's death also provided the financial ability to pursue her goal. She would apparently sink her $25,000 fortune into this task. (It's worth noting that while nearly every account tells the story this way, an 1892 *New York Sun* article claimed that she embarked on her dishwashing journey after her husband's death and that she didn't know "[e]xactly how or when [the idea] came.")

Either way, Cochrane thankfully turned out to have a knack for the mechanical. Based on her lineage, this shouldn't have been surprising as her great-grandfather earned a patent for an early steamboat design and her father was an engineer who devised a hydraulic pump for draining marshes. With the help of a friend who possessed some technical knowhow, Cochrane's initial blueprints had rows of wire compartments that could hold plates, saucers and cups. These items were then fastened around the outside of a wheel located on a copper boiler, which shot out soapy water onto the soiled dinnerware. It wasn't as fancy as a GE Profile, but it got the job done. Cochrane patented it in 1889 and the machine was the toast of the 1893 Chicago World's Fair, capturing an award for "the best mechanical construction, durability, and adaptation to its line of work."

Despite being conceptually impressive, the dishwasher was not an immediate hit with the paying public. One problem was that many households in the early twentieth century couldn't generate enough scalding hot water to run the contraption. (Also hard water, which contains various dissolved minerals, couldn't properly get the early soap sufficiently sudsy.)

A more interesting stumbling block had to do with Cochrane's inspiration. The aristocratic inventor clearly saw dishwashing as a cumbersome chore. She and her company just assumed that middle class housewives would love the opportunity to cut it out of their workload. It turned out that such an assumption was as wrongheaded as thinking the original dishwasher was just about cleaning things. A 1915 survey found that a majority of women truly loved washing dishes as a calming routine after a day full of more backbreaking tasks like cleaning laundry.

Undeterred, Cochrane's company (which would ultimately merge with the folks who made KitchenAid appliances) would change tack. As hot water became more plentiful, they sold the dishwasher on its ability to use water too hot to be handled by hand. Advertising for the machine heralded that not only did this clean dishes better, but it also killed more germs. Still, it wasn't until the postwar era of convenience that the dishwasher became a worldwide phenomenon and the every-day woman learned to value the autonomy that comes from machine-washed dinnerware.

Linoleum: Bedroom paint can

If you've been to your grandmother's home or watched reruns of classic shows like *Leave it to Beaver* or *Happy Days*, you're bound to have come across linoleum. The once-ubiquitous floor covering—popular because it was durable and relatively easy to clean—became commonplace in American kitchens in the early and mid-twentieth century.

In the 1840s, chemists were laboring to invent a substance that could do what linoleum would eventually offer. A sturdy rug-like material called "floorcloth" was already popular among the wealthy, but a more comprehensive flooring was proving elusive. Some came up with options, but they always proved too costly or not quite right. In the mid-1850s, Frederick Walton may have been aware of some of these experiments. The son of a successful engineer in Manchester, England, Walton had conducted his own scientific investigations—though in a different area (he'd patented a rubber item that could be used in the process of making cotton).

Walton's life would dramatically shift directions due to the odd fact that he kept a can of paint in his bedroom. History doesn't explain why he did this (maybe he was inspired by the fumes or wanted to be ready for that special moment when he'd get the call to be handy). Whatever the case, the can made all the difference. One day he entered his bedroom and noticed a thin film had formed on the top of the paint. His mind began to wander as he peeled the rubbery substance away. Thinking the dried linseed oil–based paint might make a good waterproofing substance, he began doing research. In 1860 he earned his first patent for linoleum.

Not everyone was initially enthused by his discovery. Wrote Walton in his autobiography: "[F]ull of my imaginative impulse and really believing that I was in possession of something of importance, I said to my Father, 'I intend to go to London and make my fortune.' He replied somewhat sarcastically, 'I suppose you think you may become Lord Mayor of London.'"

Walton didn't rise to political prominence, but he did become a successful manufacturer of his new flooring, which was also known as "resilient floor." Its combination of oxidized linseed oil with cork dust and resin on a flax backing quickly spread throughout England. (Geek note: Linoleum was named for a Latin combination of *linum* (flax) and *oleum* (oil).)

But it took another unforeseen turn to get linoleum into the homes of the Beav, the Fonz, and everyone else on the US side of the Atlantic. America became a fan of the material, in large part, because of a former Pittsburgh, Pennsylvania, clerk named Thomas Armstrong. At twenty-four years old, Armstrong was ambitious and wanted more than just working for a bottle manufacturer. In 1860 he decided to take on a partner and invest his life savings into a $300 machine that made cork stoppers. Initially, he kept his post at the bottle company just in case, but after a while the business thrived, becoming the world's largest cork company by the mid-1890s. All went well for years, until the rise in popularity of the mason jar (with its screw-on lid) began killing Armstrong's business.

Armstrong was forced to come up with an alternative for his beloved cork. He must have been thrilled when he came across linoleum, which required a lot of his product. He threw his business in that direction and, in 1909, the company began selling its own brand of the flooring. While there were other American linoleum manufacturers at the time, it was the Armstrong company's aggressive advertising and bright designs that propelled the surface material to popularity in the United States. Initially it was used throughout buildings, but thankfully for those who question the depths of linoleum's aesthetic value, it eventually became the primary domain of kitchens and bathrooms.

Matches: Unplanned friction

The greatest accidental discovery in the world of food (and beyond) has to be fire. Though there is no written history on this one, it's likely a caveman—or woman—saw a flash of lightning strike a tree or an animal, creating a flame, and, praise be, humanity realized there was an element that could keep you warm and cook your meat. At some early point, these far-off ancestors figured out how to control this magic substance by creating sparks and utilizing tinder and flint. Sizzling steaks for everyone!

But improving on this early fire creation was something that took thousands of years to do. The Romans used sulfur to help in the laborious process of getting a stone to start a fire and the Chinese also employed a match forerunner. In the seventeenth century, scientists discovered that phosphorous combined with sulfur was an even better combination for easily sparking a flame. The problem: It was nearly impossible to control.

A friction match, a small stick of wood that could be set alight in a maintainable manner by simply rubbing it against an object, was needed to ease the process of fire-starting. John Walker, a chemist and druggist from the northern English town of Stockton-upon-Tees, likely knew this. He'd been described as a "walking encyclopedia" by contemporaries, and supposedly only went into what was the precursor to the pharmacy business because, although he was trained as a surgeon, he was a bit squeamish about blood.

The most whimsical story about how Walker happened upon the first friction match in the mid-1820s has him using a stick to mix a brew featuring (for a reason lost in time) such fun chemicals as antimony sulfide, potassium chlorate, gum, and starch. These elements annoyingly coalesced together at the end of the piece of wood. Wanting to clean off his stick, he rubbed it against a hard surface and from it sprung a nice controlled flame. A more likely explanation may have been a bit more bumbling. An 1851 northern English journal simply put it this way: "By the accidental friction on the hearth of a match dipped in the mixture, a light was obtained."

Walker knew what he'd found. In 1827, he began selling a small box of fifty of his matches with a piece of sandpaper. He named his invention "Congreves" after a rocket developed by Sir William Congreve earlier in the century (still, they were often known as "Lucifer matches").

One thing Walker didn't do was patent his invention and within a decade of his discovery others were claiming to be its creator. In France, Dr. Charles Sauria was even bestowed with a medal in 1831 for his form of friction match. (Sauria's kind used white phosphorous, which did cut down on the smell produced by Walker's Congreves.)

Still, I'm not sure anyone would want to take too much credit for the original friction match. The chemicals employed in their production were highly dangerous. Interaction with white phosphorous could lead to a number of fatal bone disorders. There were horrible stories of small children getting ahold of matches and becoming gravely ill after sucking on them.

It wasn't until the 1844 invention of safety matches—which got rid of white phosphorous and placed many of the necessary chemicals on the striking surface rather than the match—that society could really enjoy the warm glow of the fire-inducing stick.

Microwaves: Melting candy bar

The venerated scientist Louis Pasteur once said, "In the field of observation, chance favors only the prepared mind." If ever there was a man who embodied the spirit of Pasteur's words it was microwave inventor Percy L. Spencer. He was a man who was always ready because his background gave him little margin for error.

Born in 1894 in the remote rural community of Howland, Maine, Spencer faced hardship from the beginning. His father died when he was just eighteen months old and his mother left him not long after. His aunt and uncle took over rearing duties, but, again, tragedy struck: His uncle passed away when Spencer was just seven years old.

Focusing on education was not an option. Spencer left school at the age of twelve to work at a spool mill. A naturally curious person, Spencer would not be consigned to a drab life in a factory. Four years later he got a job as one of three men installing electricity in the local paper mill. It didn't matter he knew nothing about the process; he simply applied a trial-and-error approach to get the plant up-and-running with electricity. In 1912 when the *Titanic* sunk, he was captivated by the story of the ship's wire operator's efforts to get word to rescue ships. Spencer joined the navy and vowed to learn about the newfangled technology. He read textbooks at night during guard duty to get up to speed.

After his hitch in the navy, he went to work at a wireless company where he was renowned for staying up all night trying to figure out how things worked. This approach, which Spencer called "solving my own situation," eventually landed him at Raytheon, Inc. At the start of World War II, the British were trying to develop radar that could help track Nazi aircraft—particularly at night. The key to their efforts was something called "magnetron tubes," which were used for the radar's microwave system. Spencer listened intently when the British explained how they were having problems with the construction of the tubes and came up with a solution that increased production dramatically and earned Raytheon a huge contract.

All this was a prelude to his biggest invention. One day in 1946, Spencer, who by now was running a division with approximately 5,000 employees, went to do an ordinary check on some of his tubes. As he attentively did his rounds, he noticed something heating up in his pocket. It was a peanut candy bar and it was beginning to melt. According to a 1958 *Reader's Digest* article, Spencer wasn't the first scientist at Raytheon to experience the melting phenomenon near the magnetron tubes, but his prepared mind made him the first to seriously investigate why it was happening.

To further test the tubes, Spencer sent an assistant out to a local store to pick up a bag of popcorn kernels. He exposed the bag to a magnetron and the popcorn burst out of the container light and fluffy. For any couch potato who has used the microwave solely for quick-popping before a game on TV, you can now say you're following in the footsteps of greatness.

Spencer would continue his work on what he dubbed the "radar range," constructing a prototype for $100,000. Needless to say, at that cost, suburban families weren't lining up to buy one. Prices began coming down in the 1950s, with a company called Tappan rolling out a home option in 1955 for a still-pricey $1,295. With so few on the market, manufacturers had a hard time getting food makers to use packaging appropriate for microwaves (for example, they couldn't stop tinfoil packaging, which we know is a microwave no-no). But over time, as more and more married couples found both partners busy in the workforce, the speed and ease of the microwave caused change. In 1967 approximately 10,000 magnetron ovens were sold; by 1975 that number reached 840,000. At the dawn of the twenty-first century, more than 93 percent of all kitchens had a microwave.

Despite nothing more than a grammar school education, Spencer changed the way Americans eat by paying attention to an accidentally melting candy bar. As one M.I.T. scientist told *Reader's Digest*, "The educated scientist knows many things won't work. Percy doesn't know what can't be done."

Paper Towels: Mistaken delivery

Clarence and E. Irvin Scott were extremely shrewd businessmen. After starting humbly in 1879 pushing a street cart around Philadelphia selling scratch pads, wrapping paper, and paper bags to merchants, the brothers boldly entered an industry that truly unnerved the sensibilities of most of their Victorian-era brethren: toilet paper. Not only did they make the concept palatable to the masses by pressing the health benefits of the disposable tissue but they also invented the toilet roll, which made using the soft paper all the easier.

No doubt, inventing the toilet paper roll should put the Scotts in some sort of pantheon, but the family wasn't done with just that wonderful creation. Business acumen did not skip a generation in the Scott clan as E. Irvin's son Arthur was every bit as nimble as his father and uncle when it came to making the most of paper products.

With the company humming along in 1907, Arthur was forced to clean up a big mistake. One day his suppliers sent along a large shipment of paper that was wholly inappropriate for bathroom use. As *Time* magazine explained in 1938, the company had received "a carload of paper too crunchy for toilet use." Arthur immediately knew this wouldn't do. After all, the company focused intently on quality. They would later spend heavily on ad campaigns touting this fact, including one stressing the "harsh tissue dangers" of competitors and another featuring a little girl complaining about an alternative brand that "scratches awful, mummy."

As a result, the initial inclination was to simply send it back. But Arthur remembered a story he'd heard about a local teacher who during a major flu epidemic wanted to do away with cloth towels at her school because she found them too unhygienic. Instead of complaining to his supplier, Arthur opted to keep the crunchy paper. He added perforations and wrapped it around one of his magic cardboard rolls (albeit a little longer than the toilet paper type).

At this point, he wasn't thinking about the kitchen. Instead, he saw his invention's public applications. He dubbed the new rolls "SaniTowels" and sold them to schools, hotels, railroad stations, and restaurants as a more sanitary way to dry hands after a bathroom pit stop. Interestingly, despite the Scotts' great acumen, the paper towel didn't migrate to the kitchen until 1931—four years after Arthur's untimely death at age fifty-one. Renamed "ScotTowels" (now known as Scott Paper Towels), these rolls of 200 sheets sold at a reasonable twenty-five cents, making it as easy to keep the kitchen clean as the company's toilet paper made it simple to keep a person's . . . well, you get the picture.

Saran Wrap: After-hours lab worker

Saran Wrap inventor Ralph Wiley deserves a prize for making the most out of a mundane job. In 1933 Wiley, a bright guy in his early twenties, had a really blah gig. He was responsible for cleaning laboratory glassware at Dow Chemical Company. One evening the monotony of the work was broken up by an odd discovery. No matter how hard he tried, he simply couldn't get one of the beakers clean.

Now, many low-rung workers might have just hidden or thrown away the beaker. After all, who counts them all? But Wiley was intrigued. He found out that the film was a by-product of a substance used in dry cleaning bearing the tongue-twisting name *perchloroethylene*. Wiley's interest was further piqued when he couldn't find a single chemical that could break it down.

Despite his excitement at turning his washing role into something bigger (he would go on to be a longtime Dow research scientist), Wiley wasn't really sure what to do with his find. Showing his age, he dubbed his glass-cleaning discovery "eonite" after an indestructible material featured in the *Little Orphan Annie* comic strip. At the time, the substance was not the type of material you'd wrap food in. Called polyvinylidene chloride by more serious Dow employees, it was smelly, greasy, and sported an ugly green hue.

At first, Wiley, who wasn't enthusiastic about the substance's prospect as a film, broke down the plastic material into fibers. Dow found a use for it in this form as part of car seat covers. But this product ended up being a loser because the fibers built up too much static electricity, shocking passengers. Next up, one of his bosses considered adding it to the construction of battery casings because it was resistant to acids. That idea didn't pan out either. Wiley grew so attached to his eonite that when Dow bigwigs considered dropping research on it because the material wasn't paying big dividends, Wiley threatened to quit.

His ploy worked and after ten years of tinkering with it, Dow finally found a decent application. A film was created and sold to the military during World War II. The wrap proved to be a handy way to bind equipment being transported by sea, protecting it from the corrosion of sea water.

But the military success didn't save Wiley's pride and joy for long. After the war, Dow sold the film to two former employees who set up a new business called the Saran Wrap Company. These guys helped refine Saran Wrap into its thin, clear (odor-free) form, and by 1949 they were marketing it for kitchen use. "It sold like hotcakes because women liked to put it over bowls," Wiley told a journalist in 1994. No fools, Dow execs bought back Saran Wrap a few years later, turning it into a huge profit maker.

While Wiley worked on many projects in his forty-two years at Dow, Saran Wrap held a special place in his heart. "It pops into my mind every time I go by the [grocery] shelf," he said. "I get a little flash of pride."

S.O.S Pads: Desperate door-to-door salesman

Being a door-to-door salesman is a tough job. Edwin Cox lived that reality when he worked the San Francisco area in the 1910s. He had what he thought was a good product: Wear-Ever Aluminum cookware. His problem was he struggled to get many housewives to let him into their kitchens to show how these lightweight rustproof pots and pans were vastly superior to other options on the market.

Cox figured if he could give them something extra he would get in the door. His company Wear-Ever would commonly offer an "inducement" to lure people to demonstrations at stores. This would come in the form of a special discount for its goods. Cox had a different, more tangible idea.

Despite all of the aluminum-ware's pluses—they didn't scorch food and stirring was not necessary when heating liquids—the cookware could become blackened by coal-fueled stoves common in that day. Cox believed that if he could offer a useful (but inexpensive) cleaning tool to hesitant housewives, he'd see sales skyrocket.

In 1917 he began working on his freebee. Steel-wool Brillo pads were patented four years earlier, but a big complaint in the cleaning process was being able to get these abrasive aids really soapy. Cox began hand-soaking little steel-wool pads in buckets full of soapy water. He would let the pad dry and then repeat. Once the small woolly squares were completely saturated in soap, he'd dry them one more time. He then found, when moistened, his invention oozed soap—perfect when it came time to clean pots and pans.

Cox hit the streets again with his product and new pads. As much as he believed in Wear-Ever, it didn't take long for him to realize that it was his steel wool that enamored potential customers. He would give one free sample of his new product to those who purchased cookware, but began getting calls to find out where additional pads could be purchased.

As a salesman, Cox recognized his new creation was the hot ticket. The next big question was what to name it. He asked his wife, who, the legend goes, suggested calling them S.O.S. pads. The acronym would stand for "save our saucepans" and would also be a reminder of the international Morse code distress signal. He loved it, but had to deal with one hiccup: He couldn't trademark S.O.S. because of its use in international communication. As a result, he tweaked the name ever so slightly, simply dropping the last period and naming it the S.O.S pad.

Stainless Steel: From gun contract to utensils

Over time regular steel corrodes. Think of old orange-tinged railroad tracks weathered and rusted by years in the sun and the rain. For centuries this fact of life also meant bad news for the everyday use of knives, forks, and spoons. Before the beginning of the twentieth century, cutlery was generally made of carbon steel, which, when air-dried, developed an unsightly reddish tinge.

Of course, utensils were pretty inconsequential compared to other steel-based items like, say, buildings and ship hulls, that could lead to even bigger headaches when rust set in. These larger concerns led many nineteenth-century scientists to search for a way to prevent the corrosion that so badly damaged the metal.

Harry Brearley was not one of those scientists. A metallurgist who ran a laboratory in his hometown of Sheffield, England, he had other metal-related issues to attend to. In 1912, with World War I on the horizon, Brearley earned a contract with a small arms manufacturer to focus on gun barrels. Rather than the corrosion that impacted cutlery and utensils, the trouble with these metal barrels was *erosion*. The constant firing of the weapons wore down the metal and required them to be replaced.

Brearley went to work experimenting with different alloys (combinations of steel and other elements) that could solve the erosion problem. On August 13, 1913, the scientist made a metal that was 12.8 percent chromium and 0.24 percent carbon. Unknowingly, this formula would change the food world. From there mythmakers take over a bit. Some say that he thought the new steel was a waste and threw it in the garbage. Later, he noticed that it hadn't rusted and took it out for further experimentation.

A more likely explanation, according to the British Stainless Steel Association, is Brearley etched the alloy with nitric acid—something he likely did with all the combinations he came up with—to assess its resistance to chemical attack. Nitric acid is a very powerful oxidizing agent. In a sense it replicates what it would be like for a knife or fork to be left out in the elements for a long time. Brearley was taken aback to find his chromium-carbon combo was highly resistant to the acid.

Now many other scientists during this period, including ones from Germany, Poland, and the United States, have argued that they were the first to independently come up with rust-repelling steel. But two facts do not appear in dispute: Brearley's material was the first to be dubbed "stainless steel" and he was the first to come up with the idea of applying it for use with eating.

Neither of these happened overnight. In a decision that probably later led to a lot of high-level firings, the bosses at his laboratory balked at the idea of using the new alloy for cutlery. Brearley was undeterred. He was in the right location to find a good utensil maker. His native Sheffield had been the center of cutlery making in England since at least the seventeenth century. Brearley approached a local cutler named R. F. Mosley with what he called "rustless steel." After some testing, Mosley loved the product. The new knives, forks, spoons, saucepans, and countless other kitchenware were shiny, easy to wash, and most important, rust-resistant. Still, he insisted on the more marketable name, stainless steel.

Styrofoam: Wartime insulator

For environmentalists, expanded polystyrene (aka Styrofoam) may be this book's most annoying accidental discovery.

During World War II, a twenty-five-year-old scientist at Dow Chemical Company named Ray McIntire wasn't thinking about a way to develop coffee cups or hamburger containers. He was aiming at coming up with a synthetic alternative to latex rubber that could serve as a sturdy flexible insulator. As part of his efforts, the inexperienced McIntire made a mistake when combining a petroleum by-product called styrene with a volatile liquid known as isobutylene. He was supposed to go easy on the isobutylene, but measured the ratio incorrectly, adding too much of the unstable matter.

After putting the combo under extreme pressure, the result was not the flexible rubber substitute he'd been hoping for. Instead, it was a rigid, exceptionally lightweight foam that had bulked up thirty times greater than what McIntire expected. Moreover, it was tremendously sturdy, extremely buoyant, and an excellent insulator. It hadn't been what McIntire had been looking for, but the young scientist figured out practical applications for the finding.

Patented in 1944, Styrofoam was adopted by the US Coast Guard, which used it in life rafts and other flotation devices. Following the war, the most popular civilian application for Styrofoam was as an insulator in home building. But as other plastic companies started producing their own versions, Styrofoam migrated into the world of food. As a great insulator, it was perfect for both ice chests and coffee cups. It also didn't easily get scalding hot so it made sense for picnic plates and fast-food packaging. It helped that it was extremely inexpensive to produce as well. (Geek note: Most squeaky takeout containers or white trays are not Styrofoam; the term—like "Kleenex" for tissue paper—is often used incorrectly to represent material created by other companies that is similar to, but not the same as, McIntire's invention.)

But for all its low-price convenience, the light-as-a-feather product can be an environmental nightmare. Its hard-wearing structure is great when you're packing leftovers, but it also makes Styrofoam-esque disposable items nearly impossible to break down at landfills. This realization came in full focus in the 1980s, when Green groups fought McDonald's over the clamshell polystyrene boxes used for their hamburgers. In 1990 the fast-food giant got the message and did away with the packaging.

Still, the plastic foam unintentionally innovated by McIntire remains omnipresent. For example, one Boston school principal said in 2010 that his cafeteria uses 72,000 lunch trays made from the material a year. As for McIntire's legacy, Dow has tried hard to keep it clear of the pollution issue, emphasizing that *real* Styrofoam (as opposed to other companies' hardened foam) is used primarily in building and never finds its way to local garbage dumps.

Tea Bags: Sample packaging

Though tea is considered a national drink in Great Britain, it was an American who revolutionized how it's used, doing so—inadvertently—in the name of capitalism. In 1908 (some say it was 1904) Thomas Sullivan was a wholesaler in New York searching for ways to cut down on his bottom line. One outlay he was finding particularly tiresome was the cost of tins used to mail tea samples to customers. To streamline expenses, he decided to try wrapping samples into sleek silk sachets.

The new packaging puzzled some recipients. Instead of opening up the small envelopes, pouring its contents into water, and sampling the tea as Sullivan had intended, a number of store owners decided to dip the bag directly into their boiling pots. For most people at this point, tea leaves were painstakingly measured and then placed in a strainer, providing flavor as hot water was poured through it into a mug. But those who tried Sullivan's tea bags loved them and wrote the wholesaler asking for more pouches (but offering suggestions on how to improve its design). A stunned Sullivan wasn't one to disappoint customers and went to work on new designs—in particular replacing the silk with less expensive gauze. Not only did this help the tea infuse the water better but it was also a financially sound maneuver.

From there a San Francisco manufacturer named Joseph Krieger refined the bag and began successfully selling his variation commercially to restaurants and hotels in 1919. Americans embraced the new way to drink tea. After all, Yanks did have a love-hate relationship with old-school tea; check your encyclopedia under the heading "Boston Tea Party."

In contrast, the Brits were not so thrilled at Sullivan's discovery. For decades after its invention, the British stuck to tradition and avoided bags. It wasn't until 1953 that a prominent British tea maker, Joseph Tetley and Company, began offering them. Their initial efforts were not good. By the early 1960s only 3 percent of tea was being purchased in bags.

But Tetley continued to advertise heavily, appealing to both the pocketbook (they pointed out that a cup of tea cost less than a penny when it came in a tea bag) and to customers' busy lifestyles (tea bags were quick and easy to use compared to measuring out tea leaves). Tetley's efforts combined with additional innovations to the packet turned the British around. Today, 96 percent of tea in the United Kingdom comes via tea bags. That equates to 130 million cups of tea consumed *every day* via Sullivan's invention.

Teflon: Guinea pig, refrigerator coolant, and fishing gear

The invention of everyone's favorite nonstick cooking material, Teflon, is a remarkable example of a series of fortunate moments. Without any of them, our eggs might still be sticking to the frying pan and pundits would have needed another nickname for "Teflon president" Ronald Reagan.

It all begins with Teflon's inventor, Roy J. Plunkett. An Ohio native, Plunkett graduated from Manchester College in 1932. He went out into the world to look for a job, but his timing couldn't have been worse. It was the height of the Depression and he couldn't find work anywhere. Left without options, he decided to go to Ohio State University and pursue a PhD in chemistry. By the time he was finished in 1936, the pains of the economy had lessened and Plunkett found a position at DuPont. His job was to come up with a nontoxic compound to cool refrigerators; he looked to fluorocarbons to reach his goal.

The fact that Plunkett would even consider the odorless, nonflammable, and nontoxic fluorocarbon as a basis for his experiments was thanks to some luck a decade earlier. In 1928 two Frigidaire scientists, Thomas Midgely Jr. and Albert Henne, were the first to consider a fluorocarbon mix, called antimony trifluoride, as a gas to keep refrigerators cool. The chemical was extremely rare. In fact, the scientists ordered five one-ounce bottles, which represented the complete supply in the United States at the time.

Their plan was to place a guinea pig in a bell jar and pump in the gas to see how it reacted to the chemical. They

picked one of the five vials of the fluorocarbon substance at random and did the experiment. They were thrilled when the little animal was unscathed by the gas. Just to double check, they took another bottle of the chemical and tried again. Much to their astonishment (and the guinea pig's horrible luck), the small animal died. It turned out that four of the five bottles contained water, which led to the production of a deadly gas called phosgene. By chance, the first bottle didn't have any water. If they'd picked one of the water-tainted bottles to start, Midgely and Henne might have deemed fluorocarbons unsafe and moved on.

Instead, Plunkett had the chemical he needed for his experiments. On April 6, 1938, Plunkett was running tests with a fluorocarbon compound called tetrafluoroethylene when something strange happened. He opened a tank in which he was doing his work and no gas came out. The tank's weight suggested that something should be in the container. "Instead of discarding this tank and getting another to continue his refrigerant research, Plunkett decided to satisfy his curiosity about the 'empty' tank," wrote Royston M. Roberts in his book *Serendipity: Accidental Discoveries in Science*. First he ran a wire through the valve to make sure it wasn't faulty. Then he cut to the chase and sawed the tank open. Inside was a white waxy powder. This polymer (a combo of gases that turn into a solid) wasn't going to help cool refrigerators, but Plunkett decided he should check whether it might have other uses. The polymer's properties proved pretty amazing. It was smooth, but wasn't dissolvable and couldn't be damaged by acids, bases, or heat.

It was also very expensive to produce, which brings us to another lucky element to this story: World War II. American military personnel involved in developing the first atomic bomb (aka The Manhattan Project) needed a substance with Teflon's exact qualities to create a gasket that could withstand an ultratoxic uranium gas used in the bomb. The army said that cost was no issue, so development of Teflon —which otherwise might have been cost-prohibitive—continued through the war.

Long after the hostilities ceased, Teflon found a home in our kitchens. In 1954, a French engineer named Marc Gregoire was the first to patent a Teflon coating for frying pans, but that wasn't his original plan. He just wanted to use a bit of Teflon to coat fishing gear. He thought it would help avoid tangling. Luckily, his wife Colette suggested that the material might be good for coating her cooking pan. He heeded his wife's wishes and the result was kitchen magic.

Indestructible when it came to a nuclear bomb, this initial Teflon-coated kitchenware did have a foe it couldn't beat: the scouring pad, which would scrape the Teflon off in the early days. Today, these pots and pans are far more durable, but they would have never gotten this far if not for the Depression, World War II, a curious scientist, an insightful housewife, and, let us not forget, a doomed guinea pig.

Acknowledgments

As is the case with most endeavors, this book could not have been completed without the help of numerous people. Thanks must begin with my fantastic friend Dan Snierson and my editors at Globe Pequot Press, Katie Benoit and Julie Marsh, for offering expert advice on what I've written. Their help was vital in this process. I'm equally grateful for the illustrations provided by David Cole Wheeler, which added so much to this effort. In terms of research, there were two websites that proved particularly valuable in the beginning when I was forming my list of accidental discoveries and unexpected inspirations: Lynne Olver's www.foodtimeline.org and Linda Stradley's www.whatscook ingamerica.net. To the many culinary authors who have come before me and touched on this topic, I hope that I've adequately built on your work. Finally, I must offer my greatest appreciation to my wife, Jennifer, and my kids, Miller and Becca, for being constant sources of inspiration for everything that I do.

Notes

In the main body of this book, I tried to keep references to a minimum in order to maintain some brevity. The sources for the quotes I used can be found here.

Introduction

"Luck affects … will be a fish." J. K. Hoyt, *The Cyclopedia of Practical Quotations* (London: Funk & Wagnalls Co., 1896), 702.

"were always making . . . not in quest of." Royston M. Roberts, *Serendipity: Accidental Discoveries in Science* (New York: John Wiley & Sons, Inc., 1989), IX.

"The really valuable . . . behind the appearance." Morton A. Meyers, *Serendipity in Modern Medical Breakthroughs* (New York: Arcade Publishing, 2007), 14.

Starters and Small Plates

Brown 'n Serve Rolls

"nationally famous." "Rolls You Buy, Then Bake," *Popular Science*, September 1950, 119.

Buffalo Wings

"What are these? . . . quiet and use your fingers!" Jay Rey, "The Lore of the Wings / Long Before the Fest, a Night of Discovery," *Buffalo News*, September 4, 2004, D1.

Caesar Salad

"the greatest recipe … in 50 years." Associated Press, "Creator of Caesar Salad Dressing Dies," *USA Today*, September 15, 2003, www.usatoday.com/news/nation/2003-09-15-salad_x.htm.

"One of my early remembrances … lunch at Caesar's Restaurant." Marc Lacey, "Wary Tourists Toss Aside a Chance to Taste History," *New York Times*, October 22, 2008, A-10.

"One day, my brother . . . me for mine." Rosemary Speirs, "Hail Caesar; Czar of All the Salads," *Canadian Magazine* (insert in the *Montreal Gazette*), April 6, 1973, 30.

Cobb Salad

"their watering hole" and "the most . . . in the world." Sally Wright Cobb and Mark Willems, *The Brown Derby Restaurant: A Hollywood Legend* (New York: Rizzoli International Publications, Inc., 1996), 140 and 111.

Kellogg's Corn Flakes

"I feel kind of blue . . . things look now." Paul Lukas and Maggie Overfelt, "Kellogg: Feeling Boxed In by His Brother, W. K. Kellogg Invented Corn Flakes, Only to Get Ripped Off by His Competitors. But With a Clever Ad Blitz, He Became the Champion of Breakfast," *Fortune Small Business*, April 1, 2003, http://money.cnn.com/magazines/fsb/fsb _archive/2003/04/01/341013/index.htm.

Nachos

"consisted of . . . jalapeno peppers," Andrew F. Smith (ed.), *The Oxford Companion to American Food and Drink* (New York: Oxford University Press, 2007), 210.

Tapas

"The art of *tapeo* . . . juicy gossip." Alan Davidson, Tom Jaine (eds.), *The Oxford Companion to Food* (New York: Oxford University Press, 2006), 783.

"It became customary . . . outdo the competition." Martha Stewart, "Ask Martha: Proper display, storage of snapshots is in order; Preserve memories for future generation," *Charleston Daily Mail* (West Virginia), October 14, 1998, P2D.

Main Courses

Chicken Marengo

"This battle is . . . to win another"; "three small eggs . . . some oil"; "plausible . . . sheer legend"; "You must feed . . . every battle"; and "abundance of . . . and wine." Patricia Bunning Stevens, *Rare Bits: Unusual Origins of Popular Recipes* (Athens: Ohio University Press, 1998), 92–93.

Chicken Tikka Masala

"[O]ne day . . . cream and spices." and "Chicken tikka masala . . . chicken with spices." and "It's basically . . . periodical improvisation," Dean Nelson and Jalees Andrabi, "Chicken tikka masala row grows as Indian chefs reprimand Scottish MPs over culinary origins," *Daily Telegraph* (UK), August 4, 2009, www.telegraph.co.uk/foodanddrink/5972643/Chicken-tikka -masala-row-grows-as-Indian-chefs-reprimand-Scottish-MPs-over -culinary-origins.html.

"the culinary masterpiece . . . Britain's most popular curry . . . EU Protected Designation of Origin." Early Day Motion 1911 (British Parliament), July 16, 2009.

Fettuccine Alfredo

"It was a hell of . . . had to do something." Bob Lape, "Alfredo's to toast birthday, eatery," *Crain's New York Business*, October 17, 1988, 22.

"Alfredo doesn't make . . . He achieves it." Todd Coleman, "The Real Alfredo," *Saveur*, April 13, 2009, www.saveur.com/article/Kitchen/ The-Real-Alfredo.

"'Look here . . . won the war?" Paul Hoffman, "Fettuccine—A Dish Fit For A Duchess," *New York Times*, November 1, 1981, Sec. 10, p. 9.

Filet-O-Fish

"Ray said . . . his sandwich did." and "My fish sandwich . . . saved my franchise." Paul Clark (*Cincinnati Enquirer*), "No fish story: Sandwich saved his McDonald's," *USA Today*, February 20, 2007, www.usatoday.com/ money/industries/food/2007-02-20-fish2-usat_x.htm.

French Dip Sandwich

"one day ... wanted the same." Robert Rector, "Philippe's an institution steeped in history," *San Gabriel Valley Tribune* (California), October 9, 2008.

"Mathieu inadvertently . . . more dipped sandwiches." www.philippes.com/history/.

"We don't . . . dip department." and "Who knows . . . still be around." Steve Harvey, "L.A. Then and Now; Century-old Cole's serves a slice of history; New owners added upscale touches but maintained the deliciously seedy ambience and French dip rivalry," *Los Angeles Times*, March 8, 2009, A-34.

Philly Cheesesteak

"the man who ... playing the piccolo." Bryce Crawford, "Brotherly grub: City of Philly Cheese Steak out plenty," *Colorado Springs Independent*, October 14, 2010, www.csindy.com/colorado/brotherly-grub/Content?oid=1877563.

Sandwiches

"There may have ... was the result." C. R. L. Fletcher, *Historical Portraits: 1700–1850 Part I (Vol. III of the Series)* (Oxford: Clarendon Press, 1919), 229.

"He was . . . abandoned character." J. Heneage Jesse, *Memoirs: Celebrated Etonians* (London: Richard Bentley and Son, 1875), 62.

Tempura

"I had long . . . Japanese cuisine." Takashi Morieda, "The Japanese Table," Kikkoman website, www.kikkoman.com/foodforum/thejapanesetable backissues/06.shtml.

TV Dinners

"It was very . . . for turkeys." and "a metaphor . . . annual problem," Roy Rivenburg, "A landmark idea, yes, but whose? Tracing the invention of the TV dinner opens a can, er, tray of worms," *Los Angeles Times*, November 23, 2003, E1.

"I figured . . . some attention," Associated Press, "Think of Gerry Thomas when you eat your next TV dinner," *Gazette* (Cedar Rapids, Iowa), November 17, 1999, 8A.

Desserts

Chocolate Chip Cookies

"try a lot . . . husband's favorites." and "your goal . . . and hostess." Ruth Graves Wakefield, *Toll House Tried and True Recipes* (New York: Dover Publications, Inc., 1977), 59.

"*no substitutes* . . . cream." and "Certainty in . . . eliminates failures." Ruth Graves Wakefield, *Ruth Wakefield's Toll House Tried and True Recipes* (New York: M. Barrows & Company, Inc., 1940), 3, 9.

Chocolate Molten Cake (Chocolate Lava Cake)

"as gracefully as . . . even riveting—meals." Frank Bruni, "Two Trailblazers, Well Down the Trail," *New York Times*, August 16, 2006, F8.

"legend . . . clean and simple." Alexandra Gill, "Where's the wow?" *Globe and Mail* (Toronto), March 25, 2009, www.theglobeandmail.com/life/article977186.ece.

"Baking one . . . miscalculated the timing." and "screaming wanting the recipe." Virginia Gerst, "This is a flop? Kitchen mistakes—like this molten chocolate cake—can live on and turn into classics with time." *Chicago Tribune*, April 26, 2006, 1 (Good Eating section).

"He was the . . . in France already." Arthur Schwartz, "Jacques Torres and Molten Chocolate Cake," April 9, 2001, www.thefoodmaven.com/diary/00000167.html.

Cookies 'N Cream Ice Cream

"Swirl, smack . . . you're looking for." Liz Van Hooser, "Meet an official taster for Edy's ice cream," *Florida Times-Union* (Jacksonville), April 2, 2009, http://jacksonville.com/lifestyles/food/2009-04-02/story/tough_on_ice_cream.

"I was in . . . invented by accident." Tracy Rasmussen, "Way cookie crumbled gave birth to hit flavor," *Reading Eagle* (Pennsylvania), April 30, 2001, A4.

Crêpes Suzette
"I was only 16 . . . that day crêpes Suzette." and "unglamorous as . . . stand." James Bacon (Associated Press), "Accidental Flame Won World Fame," *Robesonian* (Lumberton, N.C.), April 19, 1961, 2.

"a jeweled . . . a cane," Henri Charpentier, Boyden Sparks, and Alice Waters, *Life a la Henri: Being the Memories of Henri Charpentier* (New York: Modern Library, 2001), 57,

"I only make . . . and happy diners." James Bacon (Associated Press), "Legendary Crepes Suzette Creator Dies at Age 81," *Modesto Bee* (California), December 25, 1961, A2.

Granny Smith Apples
"is nearly . . . in shipping." Roger Yepsen, *Apples* (New York: W.W. Norton & Co., 1994), 120.

Candies and Snacks

Cheese Puffs
"[w]hen streamlets . . . human consumption." US Patent #2,295,868, Patented September 15, 1942, entitled "Process for Preparing Food Products."

Chewing Gum
"It was an accident . . . something with bubbles." Abby Goodnough, "W. E. Diemer, Bubble Gum Inventor, Dies at 93," *New York Times*, January 12, 1998, www.nytimes.com/1998/01/12/us/we-diemer-bubble-gum-inventor-dies-at-93.html.

Doughnuts
"greasy sinkers"; "the first . . . mortal eyes"; and "Of course . . . we used to eat." Sally Levitt Steinberg, *The Donut Book: The Whole Story in Words, Pictures & Outrageous Tales* (North Adams, Mass.: Storey Publishing, 2004), 69.

Graham Crackers

"high-seasoned food . . . the genital passions." Ronald Bailey, "The new age of reason: is the Fourth Great Awakening finally coming to a close?" *Reason*, April 1, 2008, 32.

"enthusiastically embraced." Barbara Brown Zikmund, "The legacy of this place: Oberlin, Ohio," *Journal of Ecumenical Studies*, September 22, 2007, 499.

"Grahamites" and "poet of bran," Charles Panati, *Panati's Extraordinary Origins of Everyday Things* (New York: Perennial Library, 1987), 414.

Jelly Tots

"I didn't even . . . attention to it." and "They either hug . . . ruining their teeth." Grant Woodward, "Brian Boffey: Horsforth's own Jelly Tots inventor," *Yorkshire Post* (UK), March 9, 2009.

PEZ

"a luxury confection for wealthy people." "Austrian Cult Candy: PEZ Celebrates its 80th Anniversary With a Unique Charity Campaign!" *Medianet Press Release Wire*, October 10, 2007.

"smoking prohibited, PEZing allowed." *Food Trade Review*, March 1, 2007.

"pocket article dispensing container." US Patent #2,620,061, Patented December 2, 1952, entitled "Pocket Article Dispensing Container."

Pop Rocks

"Throughout the industry . . . one else considered"; "Carbonated candy . . . better to do?"; and "we checked . . . alive and well." Marv Rudolph, *Pop Rocks: The Inside Story of America's Revolutionary Candy* (Sharon, Mass.: Specialty Publishers LLC, 2006), 1, 21, 87.

Popsicles

"a handled frozen confection." and "I was flat . . . same since." Associated Press, "Frank Epperson, 89, Inventor of Popsicle, Dies in California," *New York Times*, October 27, 1983, www.nytimes.com/1983/10/27/obituaries/frank-epperson-89-inventor-of-popsicle-dies-in-california.html.

"It has given . . . part of it all." United Press International, "Popsicle inventor notes anniversary," *Daily Facts* (Redlands, Calif.), March 16, 1973, 2.

Potato Chips

"fit for a king . . . could contrive"; "most credible"; and "Aunt Katie . . . plenty of these." Dirk Burhans, *Crunch! A History of the Great American Potato Chip* (Madison, Wis.: Terrace Books, 2008), 16, 20–21.

Twinkies

"I shortened . . . the kids." and "Some people say . . . never hurt them." Edward Baumann, "James A. Dewar, 88; Created Twinkies Cakes," *Chicago Tribune*, July 2, 1985, C6.

"WASP Soul Food." Jerry Belcher, "Man who concocted the Twinkie dies; James A. Dewar's Treat is part of America's diet and folklore," *Los Angeles Times*, July 3, 1985, 2 (Metro section).

Additives and Extras

Ice-Cream Cone

"He actually . . . tea cups." Jim Salter (Associated Press), "Ice cream cone's birth topic of heated debate," *Grand Rapids Press* (Michigan), October 5, 2003, A5.

"Many of the . . . 100 years ago." "Centennial ode to the cone," *Chicago Tribune*, July 9, 2004, 22 (Editorial section).

Maple Syrup

"the chase"; "she might . . . the snow"; "strict compliance"; and "pleasant drink," Rowland E. Robinson, "Old-Time Sugar-Making," *Atlantic Monthly*, vol. 77 (1896), 467–68.

"picture pioneer . . . by none." Vermont Department of Agriculture, "Sugar Making by the Indians," *Bulletin*, 1914, 17.

Marmalade

"Janet Keiller . . . own marmalade." C. Anne Wilson, *The Book of Marmalade* (Philadelphia: University of Pennsylvania Press, 1999), 64.

Mayonnaise

"[E]vidently, he . . . Port Mahon." and "[T]he Richelieu . . . makes sense." Debbie Elliot, National Public Radio *(Weekend All Things Considered),* August 13, 2006.

Nutella

"Every chocolatier . . . make chocolate." Clara Ferreira-Marques (Reuters), "Turin hosts month-long feast dipped in layers of chocolate," *Star-Ledger* (Newark, N.J.), May 12, 2004, 40 (Savor section).

"famous." Alan Davidson, Tom Jaine (ed.), *The Oxford Companion to Food* (New York: Oxford University Press, 2006), 375.

"the Piedmontese . . . sweet taste." Elena Kostioukovitch, *Why Italians Love to Talk About Food* (New York: Macmillan, 2009), 96.

Whipped Cream

"Yes, the chemists . . . the housewives' cares." Kenneth T. Downs, "You Mean You Never Have Any Luck At Whipping Cream?" *Indiana Evening Gazette*, April 26, 1935, 3.

Worcestershire Sauce

"as far as . . . in India." and "We have . . . own truth." R. W. Apple Jr. (*New York Times*), "Don't ask what makes Lea & Perrins Worcestershire so special—they won't tell," *Seattle Post-Intelligencer*, August 30, 2000.

Drinks

Champagne

"The orgies . . . champagne brings." and "These phenomena . . . from happening." Don and Petie Kladstrup, *Champagne: How the World's Most Glamorous Wine Triumphed Over War and Hard Times* (New York: HarperCollins e-books, 2005), Kindle locations 589, 628.

Coca-Cola

"Someone in need . . . Pemberton's products." and "The medical properties . . . mental depression, etc." Constance L. Hays, *The Real Thing: Truth and Power at the Coca-Cola Company* (New York: Random House, 2004), 96, 100–101.

Gibson Martini

"found himself . . . cocktail parties." Irma von Starkloff Rombauer, Marion Rombauer Becker, *Joy of Cooking* (New York: Simon and Schuster, 1975), 50.

Irish Coffee

"I'm the man . . . Joe Sheridan." Foynes Flying Boat Museum website, www .flyingboatmuseum.com/irishcoffee_chef.html.

Ovaltine

"nourishing food supplement." "100 years of Ovomaltine—a power brand celebrates its centenary," *Swiss News*, October 1, 2004, 36.

"[H]e marketed . . . as it were." Nick Walker, "Alpine beverage takes root in the subtropics," *South China Morning Post*, August 1, 2006, 2 (Supplements).

"Every day . . . bright and keen." "The days when ovaltine ruled," *Bristol Evening Post* (UK), May 18, 2004, 38.

Pink Lemonade

"Pete was . . . long chances."; "There were . . . could find none"; "Without giving any . . . fine strawberry lemonade"; and "with no particular . . . a rich pink." George Conklin, Harvey W. Root, *The Ways of the Circus: Being the Memories and Adventures of George Conklin, Tamer of Lions* (New York: Harper and Brothers Publishers, 1921), 229–30.

"One day while . . . his chance discovery." "Inventor of Pink Lemonade Dead," *New York Times*, September 18, 1912.

Tea

"increasing concentration and alertness," Jane Pettigrew, *The Tea Companion: A Connoisseur's Guide* (London: Quintet Publishing Ltd., 2004), 10.

White Zinfandel

"the *TV Guide* of wines." David L. Coddon, "Over, under, sideways, down—red wine is the best in town," *San Diego Union-Tribune*, March 3, 2005, 47 (Entertainment section).

"Oh, okay . . . pronounce it." and ""I was thinking . . . making it." and "Oh, my God, it's got . . . me at the time." Tyler Colman, "Bob Trinchero on the first Sutter Home white zinfandel," Dr. Vino's wine blog, January 18, 2011, www.drvino.com/2011/01/18/white-zinfandel-sutter-home-trinchero-first-1975/.

"It's been an amazing . . . happened to me." Tim Patterson, "Cellar Scene," *Wines & Vines*, August 1, 2005, 58.

Kitchen Inventions and Innovations
CorningWare

"I figured . . . the furnace." Randolph Picht (Associated Press), "He dishes out new ideas for Corning," *Daily Intelligencer* (Doylestown, Penn.), August 1, 1986, 15A.

Dishwashers

"[e]xactly how . . . came." *New York Sun*, "Woman and Home," *Bradford Era* (Pennsylvania), April 11, 1892, 2.

"the best mechanical construction, durability, and adaptation to its line of work." Charles Panati, *Panati's Extraordinary Origins of Everyday Things* (New York: Perennial Library, 1987), 103.

Linoleum

"[F]ull of my imaginative impulse . . . Lord Mayor of London.'" Sarah Hosking, Liz Haggard, *Healing the Hospital Environment: Design, Management and Maintenance of Healthcare Premises* (New York: Routledge, 1999), 86.

Matches

"walking encyclopedia." and "By the accidental . . . light was obtained." Walter Scott, *The Monthly chronicle of North country lore and legend*, vol. 4, 1890, 147, 148.

Microwaves

"In the field . . . prepared mind." Morton A. Meyers, *Serendipity in Modern Medical Breakthroughs* (New York: Arcade Publishing, 2007), 7.

"solving my own situation." and "The educated scientist . . . what can't be done." Don Murray, "Percy Spencer and His Itch to Know," *Reader's Digest*, August 1958, 114.

Paper Towels

"a carload . . . toilet use"; "harsh tissue dangers"; and "scratches awful, mummy." "Manufacturing Tissue Issue," *Time*, August 22, 1938, www.time.com/time/magazine/article/0,9171,788421,00.html#ixzz1JFFAyp1S.

Saran Wrap

"It sold . . . over bowls." and "It pops into . . . flash of pride." Associated Press, "Saran Wrap, marking 40 years in use, began as a lab byproduct," *Toledo Blade* (Ohio), January 25, 1994, 19.

Teflon

"Instead of discarding . . . the 'empty' tank," Royston M. Roberts, *Serendipity: Accidental Discoveries in Science* (New York: John Wiley & Sons, Inc., 1989), 187.

Selected Sources and Further Reading

Lots of research went into each entry in this book, making it difficult to mention every resource utilized. But here's a list of some books broad in scope that I carefully studied for this work and that are worth perusing if you want more on food or drink in general or on this topic in particular.

American Century Cookbook: The Most Popular Recipes of the 20th Century (1997) by Jean Anderson

Beyond the Ice Cream Cone: The Whole Scoop on Food at the 1904 World's Fair (2004) by Pamela J. Vaccaro

Do Donuts Have Holes? Fascinating Facts About What We Eat and Drink (2004) by Don Voorhees

A History of Food (2009) by Maguelonne Toussaint-Samat

The New Food Lover's Companion (2001) by Sharon Tyler Herbst

On Food and Cooking: The Science and Lore of the Kitchen (2004) by Harold McGee

The Oxford Companion to American Food and Drink (2007) edited by Andrew F. Smith

The Oxford Companion to Food (2006) by Alan Davidson (edited by Tom Jaine)

Panati's Extraordinary Origins of Everyday Things (1987) by Charles Panati

Rare Bits: Unusual Origins of Popular Recipes (1998) by Patricia Bunning Stevens

Serendipity: Accidental Discoveries in Science (1989) by Royston M. Roberts

10,001 Food Facts, Chef's Secrets & Household Hints (2000) by Myles H. Bader

What Caesar Did for My Salad: Not to Mention the Earl's Sandwich, Pavlova's Meringue and Other Curious Stories Behind our Favourite Foods (2010) by Albert Jack

Index

About the Author

Josh Chetwynd is a journalist, broadcaster, and author. He's worked as a staff reporter for *USA Today*, the *Hollywood Reporter*, and *U.S. News & World Report*. His writing has also appeared in such publications as the *Wall Street Journal*, the *Times* (of London), and the *Harvard Negotiation Law Review*. He lives in Denver, Colorado, with his wife and two children and is always up for a good meal.